Simple S.I.P. Homes

Structural-Insulated-Panel-Based Practical Homes

Read This Important Safety Notice
To prevent accidents, keep safety in mind while you work. Use the safety guards installed on power equipment: they are for your protection. When working on power equipment, keep fingers away from saw blades, wear safety goggles to prevent injuries from flying wood chips and sawdust, wear hearing protection and consider installing a dust vacuum to reduce the amount of airborne sawdust in your woodshop. Don't wear loose clothing, such as neckties or shirts with loose sleeves, or jewelry, such as rings, necklaces or bracelets, when working on power equipment. Tie back long hair to prevent it from getting caught in your equipment. People who are sensitive to certain chemicals should check the chemical content of any product before using it. The author and editor who compiled this book have tried to make the contents as accurate and correct as possible. Plans, illustrations photographs and text have been carefully checked. All instruction, plans and projects should be carefully read, studied and understood before beginning construction. Due to the variability of local conditions, construction materials, skill levels, etc., the author assumes no responsibility for any accidents, injuries, damages or other losses incurred resulting from the information presented in this book.

Published by Arthur Smith

Library of Congress Control Number: 2020913720

Editor: Jim Stack
Designer: Jim Stack
Photographer: Art Smith
Illustrator: Art Smith

Intro

I first became acquainted with Art Smith when I was an editor of *Popular Woodworking Books at F+W Media, Inc.* He proposed a book about Eco-friendly and cost-effective homes. *Building Today's Green Home: Practical, cost-effective and Eco-responsible homebuilding* was the resulting book, published in 2009. Art's focus group was, and is, the baby-boomer (BB) generation (born between 1946 and 1964).

Because I am a BB, I was intrigued by Art's assertion that when BBs retire, they should consider downsizing, which means literally finding, or building, a smaller house, and thinning out all the stuff they/we accumulate over the years.

I talked with Art many times about downsizing and retirement. My wife and I downsized in 2014, a couple years after we were "asked" to retire from our respective places of employment. We moved into a ranch-style house, which has proven to be the perfect move for us. In his new book, *Simple SIP Homes: Structural-Insulated-Panel-Based Practical Homes,* Art discusses the design and practical functions of SIP-built homes. Included are detailed floor plans of a few houses that Art has designed.

In Art's two books, the reader has all the information they would need to build an Eco-friendly, off-the-grid, open-concept, exceptionally strong, and perfect retirement home.

- Jim Stack

About the author

Art Smith, Residential Designer, LEED AP, has had a special interest in energy-efficient, yet practical homes since a crucial college decision to study engineering instead of architecture. Starting with his first passive-solar home, designed in 1980 in an Atlanta suburb, to designing current client's homes, his focus is on balancing low-energy use, low-maintenance and comfortable living — particularly for the aging baby boomers. Armed with an engineering and manufacturing background. Art, and his family, escaped the Atlanta high-tech world to the north Georgia mountains in 2001 to continue this pursuit full time.

His prior firm, **Rocky Ridge Designs**, before retiring, designed and built Timber Trusses mated to specific floor plans.

REFERENCES

1. "Preface" from Homers Iliad, by Alexander Pope
2. Building with Structural Insulated Panels, by Michael Morley, Taunton Press
3. R-CONTROL SIP brochure : R-Control Building Systems, Excelsior, MN
4. www.sips.org, BASF Study shows Sips Cut Framing labor in Half", 2/13/2008
5. R-CONTROL SIP brochure : R-Control Building Systems, Excelsior, MN
6. 2006 International Residential Code, p268, 803.1
7. 2013 IECC (RESIDENTAIL ENERGY CODE)
8. MITSUBISHI ELECTRIC Submittal M-Series form: MXZ-3B24NA-1
9. The Passive Solar Energy Book, by Edward Mazria, Rodale, p402
10. The Passive Solar Energy Book, by Edward Mazria, Rodale, p138 & 139
11. Consumer Reports, August 2016
12. https://www.mikeroweworks.org/
13. https://neces.ed.gov/programs/digest/tables
14. Consumer Reports, August 2016, front cover
15. The Passive Solar Energy Book, by Edward Mazria, Rodale, p252
16. www.uscensus.gov, "Median and average Square feet…."

Photo credits:

All photos taken by the author except the following:
Rich Soukup - Fig. 1.5, 1.6, 1.7, and 1.8.

Contents

Chap 1 SIPs are the realistic leading edge - page 6

Chap 2 Starting Point: The Basic Chalet - page 26

Chap 3 Modularity - What & Why? - page 40

Chap 4 Vaulted Ranches - page 64

Chap 5 Timber TEE - page 78

Chap 6 The Winged Chalet - page 86

Chap 7 The Squashed-H - page 96

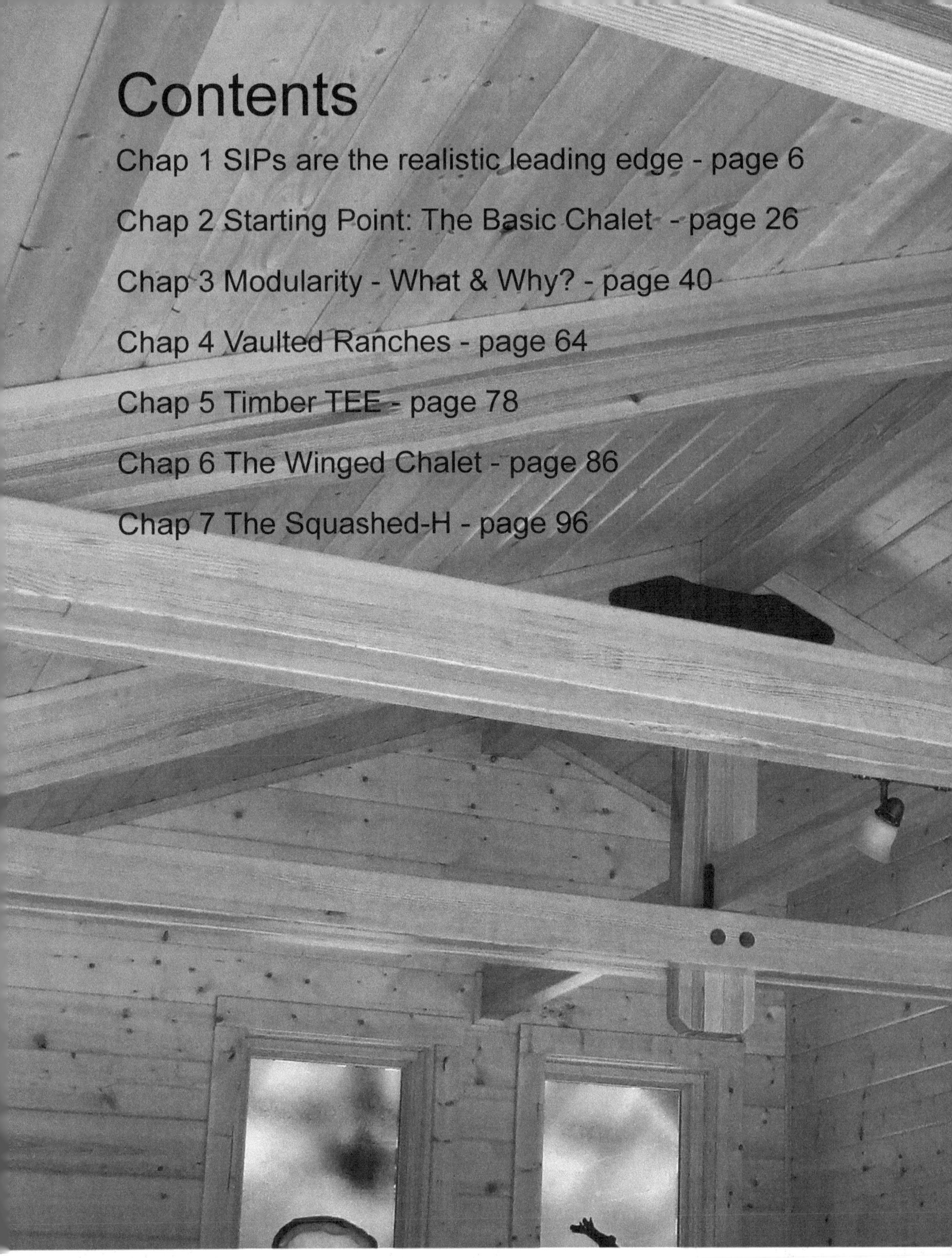

chapter one

SIPs are the realistic leading edge

Alexander Pope's quotation, "Simplicity is the mean between ostentation and rusticity", from his Preface in Homer's Iliad[1] in the eighteen century, is relevant even today. Simplicity, as stated in the title of Chapter 8 in *Today's GREEN Home: Practical, Cost-efficient, and Eco-Responsible Homebuilding*, was not just an accident. That chapter's title, "The Promise of SIPs", is significant. That is, we are missing a major opportunity for utilizing a key component for this critical, United States (U.S.) Eco-Friendly, but practical, future. SIPs (Structural Insulated Panels) have so much potential as a proven technology to build stronger, faster, and more energy-efficient homes than any other system that I have experienced (fig. 1.4). My goal in this work is to deliver my part of "The Promise". Different floor plans, of quality, yet simple-to-build homes, will be presented. Most of the walls are made entirely of SIP modules. So instead, of still digging deeper into our hole of poor quality American homes, we will climb out on the back of this terrific modular building block. What a superb manner for our U.S. technology to again exert its presence in this global energy dilemma!

OSTENTATION

As stated in *Building Today's Green Home*, the case was made that we Americans, particularly during the bulk of the baby-boomer's era, chased the "Dream Home" in what was only for appearances, without real quality of this major life purchase. Thus, ostentation, or an excessive display, was the main result. What else did we obtain? One of the world's largest melt-downs of surplus of products (homes) with excesses of appearance-only clearly demonstrated. A major by-product is the huge U.S. government bailout of an extraordinary $700 billion (that's with a "B") figure for financial firms. We and our children will pay this overdue credit card for years. But the real significance is the more than several trillion dollar loss of home values (which was substantially based on curb-appeal!). Many of us had discussed the growing debt potential by casually driving through many urban and suburban areas in the past several years, wondering who was buying all of these new upscale homes. Most families could not afford them if they had tried to buy! Figure 1.1 shows what I offer as an example of excesses. If we truly desire real quality, then we must give up this level of ostentation.

Fig. 1.1 Ostentation in action. Excessive house trim.

RUSTICITY

On the other end, away from the fancy extreme, is the more basic approach towards moderation. In *Building Today's GREEN Home*, in the "Causal Cabin/Timber Style" chapter, I discussed this syndrome of specifically having too much wood and not balancing this extreme with other colors and textures. I noticed this unbalance of decor from clients who had spent most of their recent adulthood in cramped, urban, monotone-like environments. When they finally "escaped" to the more laid-back mountain environment, they went to the opposite extreme. They desired "everything" in their new home, so rustic that even decorations made from rotting, decayed tree branch sections, potentially with insects, were gloriously displayed!

MEAN

As evidence of a balance between these two extremes, I offer only a picture: Figure 1.2 is my example of a "mean" in the middle. This is the view of our Walnut Mountain *EnergyStar* model home project's great-room timber-truss ceiling. We have the warmth of wood, balanced with colors that can be updated in time and tastes, a comfortable and realistic size, and the quality integrity confirmed by a certification process (*EnergyStar*). So, if I combine this special structural building block, SIPs, with some of the more causal, less formal, yet simple floor plan concepts, I believe we can achieve a real mean. Thus, some sanity and real value for our future American homes is within reach!

Fig. 1.2 Mean: Great room, *Energystar* model home.

FIRST-TIME HOME BUILDERS

Before we really delve into the technical specifics of building homes with SIP modules, I believe an analogy to American's second most expensive purchase (cars) will aid us in this new perspective of "modularity". So called "Custom" homes are really just prototypes. Almost every homeowner who builds their first home will attest to their eye-opening lessons of the difficult tasks involved. The first-time builders are just trying out examples of some collection of home-building ideas that may or may not work. In fact, the real test of their validity, and the real crime, lies in many years down the road; when it is too late to turn back and some or even all is wasted. Yet most only participate in one or two of those experiences in their lifetime. Thus, they still are really amateurs at even after building one home.

Now my automotive analogy: Almost any major city, or even medium-sized towns across America have a district, typically a boulevard stretch, where many of the car dealers are located. In the Atlanta Metro area, names such as Peachtree Industrial, Buford Highway, or even Cobb Parkway echo a familiar tone. This Saturday morning a couple is on a car buying expedition down one of these parkways. This couple will purchase their new vehicle in the manner that we build "custom homes". Even American manufacturers (not including my favorite, Honda) have high-volume standard models on the showroom floors that are an improved product. They are designed, built, and inspected/tested to fairly high standards (now imposed by United States government safety and pollution levels). Also, now with the realty of Global competition, their standard product is simply-pretty good.

But our buying friends want something "custom" for themselves. So, they first stop at the Dodge dealer because the husband likes the big bold Dodge Ram grill on the big trucks. The wife likes the flower holder and the shape of the new Volkswagen bug bubble shape. He likes the big Chevy V8 engine. She notes that the Honda transmission is highly rated. He likes the running board look of the one of the Ford F-150 truck models. She likes the doors of a Toyota Camry. And on and on. Can we guess how this custom collection of components will work at the end of the boulevard drive when attempting to put them together? It is "custom", but what is it? <u>It will likely never be quality.</u>

This car analogy is not far from the process of building a custom home. It's simply another American fad. The vast majority of Americans, particularly Baby-Boomers planning for later years, simply cannot afford the risk of customizing at this crucial decision juncture and still yield a quality retirement home.

If one feels that "customizing" is the link to "quality", I shall offer a paraphrased quote from one of my Green consultant business associates, Carl Seville, from the Atlanta area: "Passing Code is like getting a D minus". In other words, a typical suburban home that just passes the building code, with the focus on cosmetics (customizing), will not get you very far. Or in my way of thinking: Code is just "the minimum".

Simply put, we need more modularization in the CORE of the home to raise the overall quality beyond just a passing grade. The customizing level that does work is using a few color and minor cosmetic refinements-such as attached porches, garages, and finishes. I maintain that a more standardized core of homes built using SIPs is the best way to achieve this historically important American need: quality and economy.

I offer a series of floor plans that display a wide range of realistic sizes; Not overdone, pretentious ones. The following chapters will show important derivatives of these general plan styles that feed other rapidly growing United States housing issues (small size and low energy).

PRACTICAL FLOOR PLANS

These floor plans range from a 2bed/2bath "MINI" ranch (980sq.ft.) to an almost mid-size 3bed-2bath (1,700sq.ft.) dual, street view, gable version. Our efforts will focus generally for those that are serious, like the Baby-Boomer wave, and actively committed to downsizing into realistic, yet high-quality and comfortable-living homes. Also, we will show a transition path for most of these plans that can implement some level of passive solar energy input, which will enable the addition of active solar features as

FLOOR PLAN NAME >> FEATURES:	VAULTED RANCH (MINI)	VAULTED RANCH (MAXI)	"TEE", CHALET	"WING-ED" CHALET #2	"WING-ED" CHALET #3	SQUASHED - "H"
TRUSSES (5/12-20' PINE) >>	6	8	8	8	9	10
TOTAL FLOOR AREA >>	960 s.f.	1173 s.f.	1377 s.f.	1260 s.f.	1493 s.f.	1700 s.f.
GREAT ROOM AREA >>	427 s.f.	640 s.f.	630 s.f.	533 s.f.	640 s.f.	640 s.f.
BED/BATH LAYOUT >>	2 BED / 2 BATH	2 BED / 2 BATH	2 BED / 2 BA	2 BED / 2 BA	3 BED / 2 BA	3 BED / 2 BA
MASTER BEDROOM AREA >>	205 s.f.	205 s.f.	264 s.f.	199 s.f.	256 s.f	320 s.f.
MASTER BATH AREA >>	64 s.f.	64 s.f.	78 s.f.	58 s.f.	86 s.f.	117 s.f.
MASTER CLOSET AREA >>	52 s.f.	52 s.f.	57 s.f.	53 s.f.	79 s.f.	96 s.f.
SECOND BEDROOM AREA >>	141 s.f.	141 s.f.	176 s.f.	174 s.f.	170 s.f./132 s.f.	213 / 200 s.f.
SECOND CLOSET AREA >>	11 s.f.	11 s.f.	22 s.f.	13 s.f.	36 s.f./25 s.f.	15 / 15 s.f.
SECOND BATH AREA >>	62 s.f.	62 s.f.	57 s.f.	101 s.f	67 s.f.	53 s.f.

FIGURE 1.3 – FLOOR PLAN FEATURE MATRIX   **NOTES:** *1 – Floor area is gross square feet (s.f.), outside wall to middle of inside wall*
2- Net floor area is about 6-8% less than gross figure

desired, since these will be very energy efficient. The cost to maximize the active and passive solar elements will be even more impressive. Some plans, particularly the larger versions, will incorporate more wheelchair- friendly features, not fully ADA compliant, but as practically achievable in our desired home size.

The chart of features vs. specific floor plans, shown in Figure 1.3, will be our reference guide throughout this book. We need to establish the technical basics for these particular SIP-structured homes as shown in "The Fundamentals" chapter found in Building Today's GREEN Home. If and when you want the technical SIP building details, refer to Michael Morley's terrific book, *Building with Structural Insulated Panels*[2].

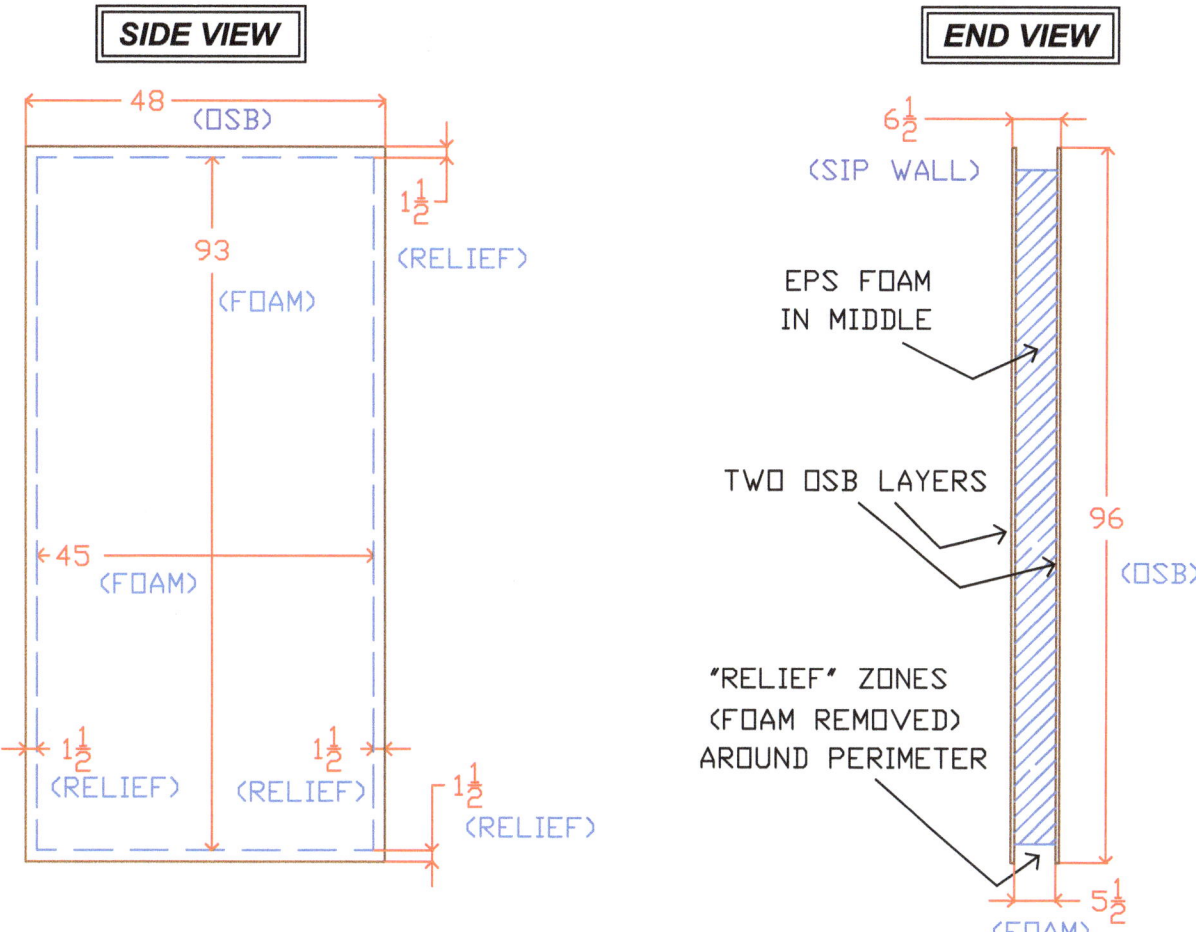

Fig. 1.4 Typical small SIP module

SIPS

In Figure 1.4 we have my "Rectangular Oreo Cookie" representation of the most base SIP panel: 4' wide by 8' high. The outer two OSB, or plywood sheets, bonded to the interior foam insulation block, enable its strength and high insulation value (R22 for EPS foam at 5-1/2" thick) in one stage. At only 4' wide, even this module size is a great building block[3].

For every 4' of a normal 8'-high wall home, you only need one panel and a couple wood interconnecting pieces. For a 48'- long wall, one needs only a dozen of these panels. The simplest, yet very strong module, uses pairs of OSB vertical splines typically at the panel connecting points or 2×6s. The 2×6 size relief zone (1-1/2" deep by 5-1/2" wide) on the top and bottoms of the SIP are for the single top and bottom plates to interconnect a line of panels to make a longer wall. One could also insert a 2×6 vertical (or two with the 1-1/2" relief zones in each panel's side insulation foam) stud, or 4×6 posts with 1-3/4" foam reliefs, for an increase in strength. However, the spliced, simply-connected wall has proven to be much stronger than the average framed-and-sheathed exterior wall.

Fig. 1.5 First corner of the building being assembled using small SIPs.

Fig. 1.6 Pre-framed window module being inserted into SIP.

Fig. 1.7 By midday, with this crew's first time SIP project, they have about one-half of the main-floor structure installed.

Fig. 1.8 The large, pre-built gable-end module is being lifted onto the SIP wall perimeter that is now completed. This taller, 12/12 Mountain Chalet (really one-and-a-half stories) results in modules much larger than the smaller 4'×8' SIPs used in the perimeter 8'-high walls. (The wall sections that are not yet covered with the OSB sheathing are pre-framed stud-type walls and will soon be sheathed.) Again, some hybrid construction is being used.

Fig. 1.9 The completed SIP walls a day later. The final few wall items were completed earlier that morning before the interior Timber Truss installation began. This first-time 3-man crew, with lots of generic framing experience, completed the final erection for the bulk of the wall structure with these smaller SIPs in about one day.

Fig. 1.10 Using slightly larger SIP modules, 6' to 16' long to construct a 1,400 sq.ft. home.

Fig. 1.11 A 4-man crew worked on this house. By mid morning, they had progressed to this point in construction. The men could shift and turn up these panels without using the boom truck support.

Fig. 1.12 By the end of the day, the crew had reached this point in the construction.

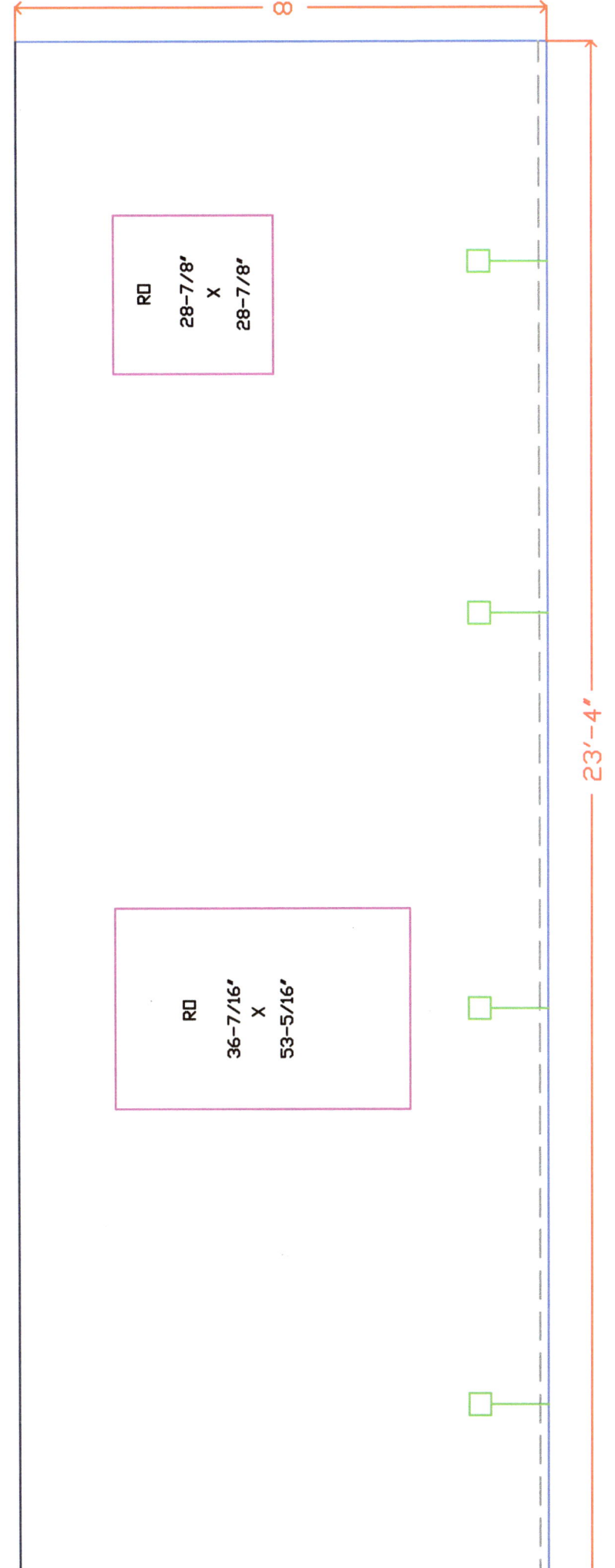

Fig. 1.13 This is a single, large SIP module that represents the length of a 24'-long traditionally-framed building.

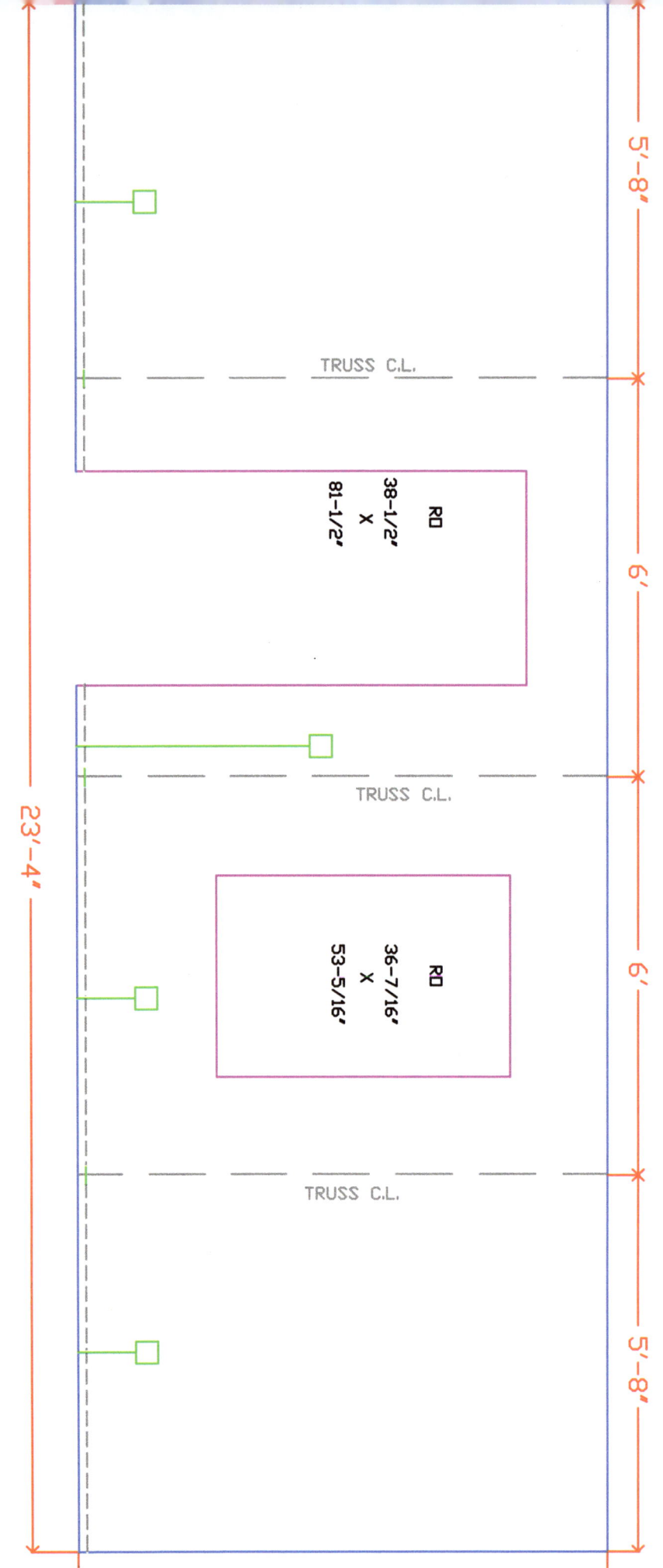

Fig. 1.14 This is another, identically sized, but differently-detailed wall, that is the other side of this Guest House. With just these two (Figs. 1.13 and 1.14) 24'-long, standard 8'-high SIP panels, more than 50% of the perimeter walls can be erected.

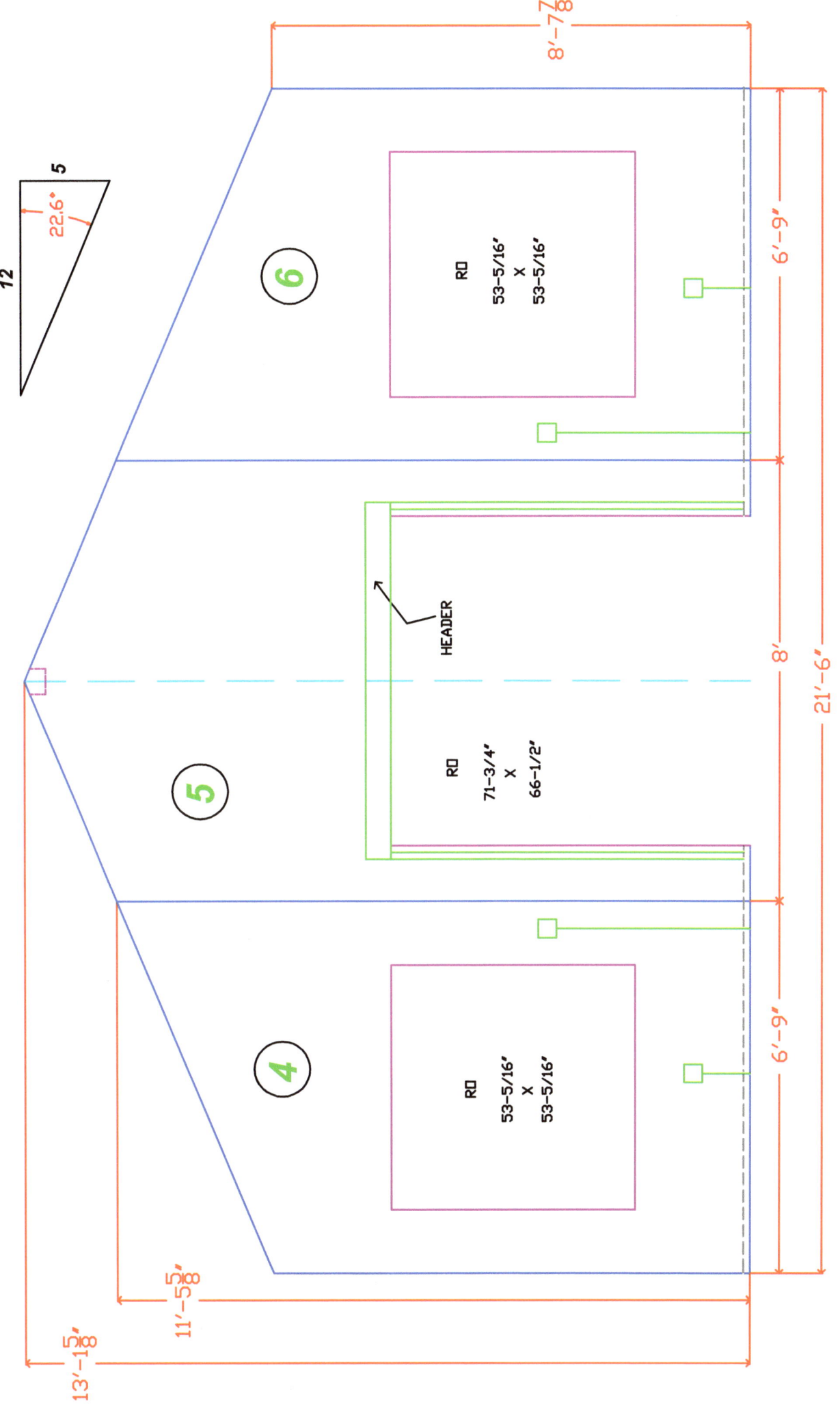

Fig. 1.15 A gable-end shop drawing showing the 3 smaller SIPs that form this full 21'-6" section. Note that these SIPs are oriented in a vertical configuration — balloon-style framing — that is, they don't have a break, or hinge point at the 8'-eave level and thus are stronger in hurricane wind zones. Since the panels are designed to mate for a 5/12 roof pitch, they are not tall and are truckable.

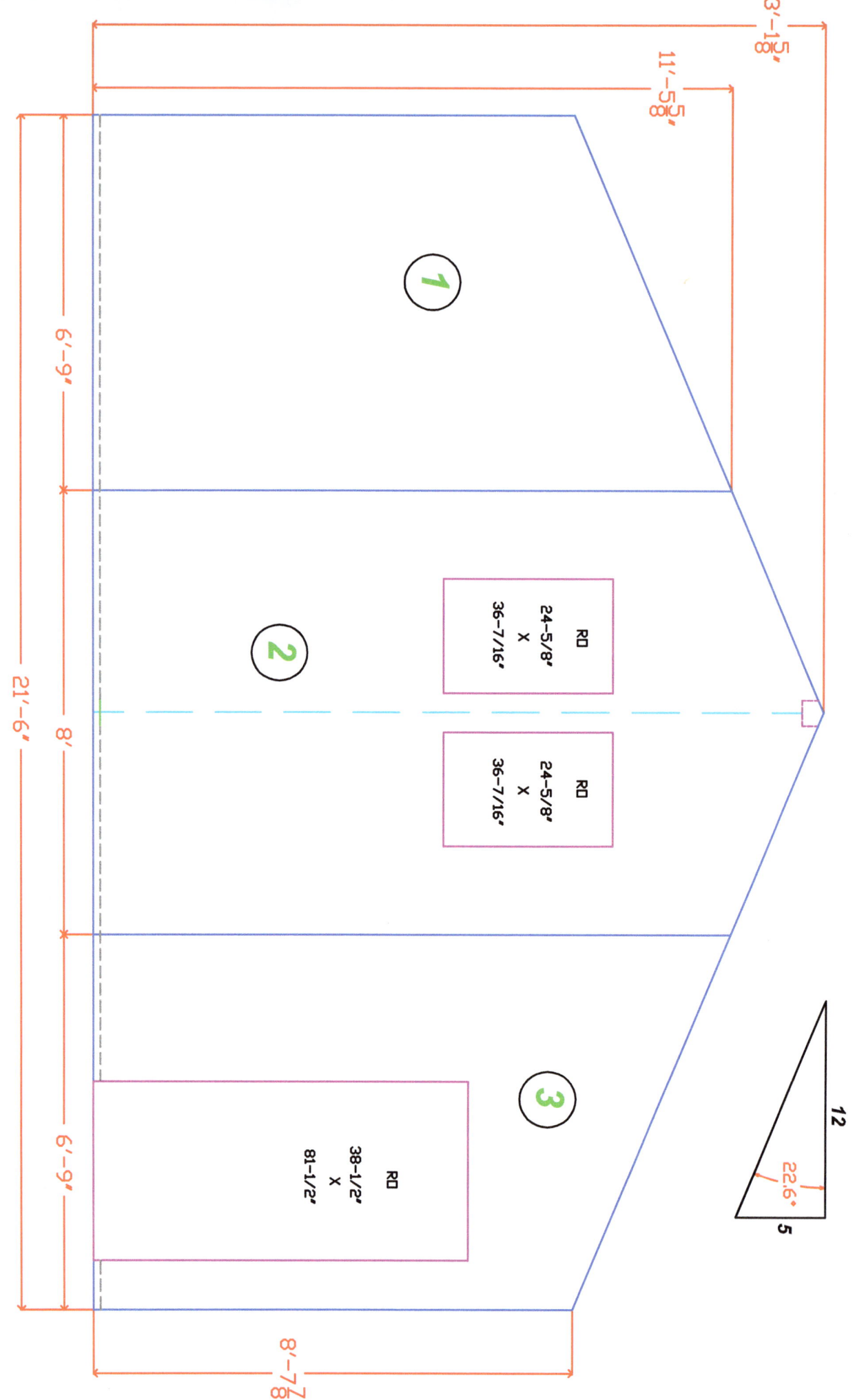

Fig. 1.16 These four (Figs. 1.13, 1.14, 1.15 and 1.16) SIP shop drawings represent the eight modules that complete the wall area of a small Guest House.

Fig. 1.17 This is the inside view of the east gable of the framed Guest House project, completed using conventional stud framing that matches the Fig. 1.15 SIP shop drawing.

Fig. 1.18 This Guest House uses modest-sized 5/12 Timber Trusses. This roof indicates that modest is not too bad after all! The client and the many visitors to this Guest House attest to the comfortable and quality feel. This design is not overblown just for volume's sake.

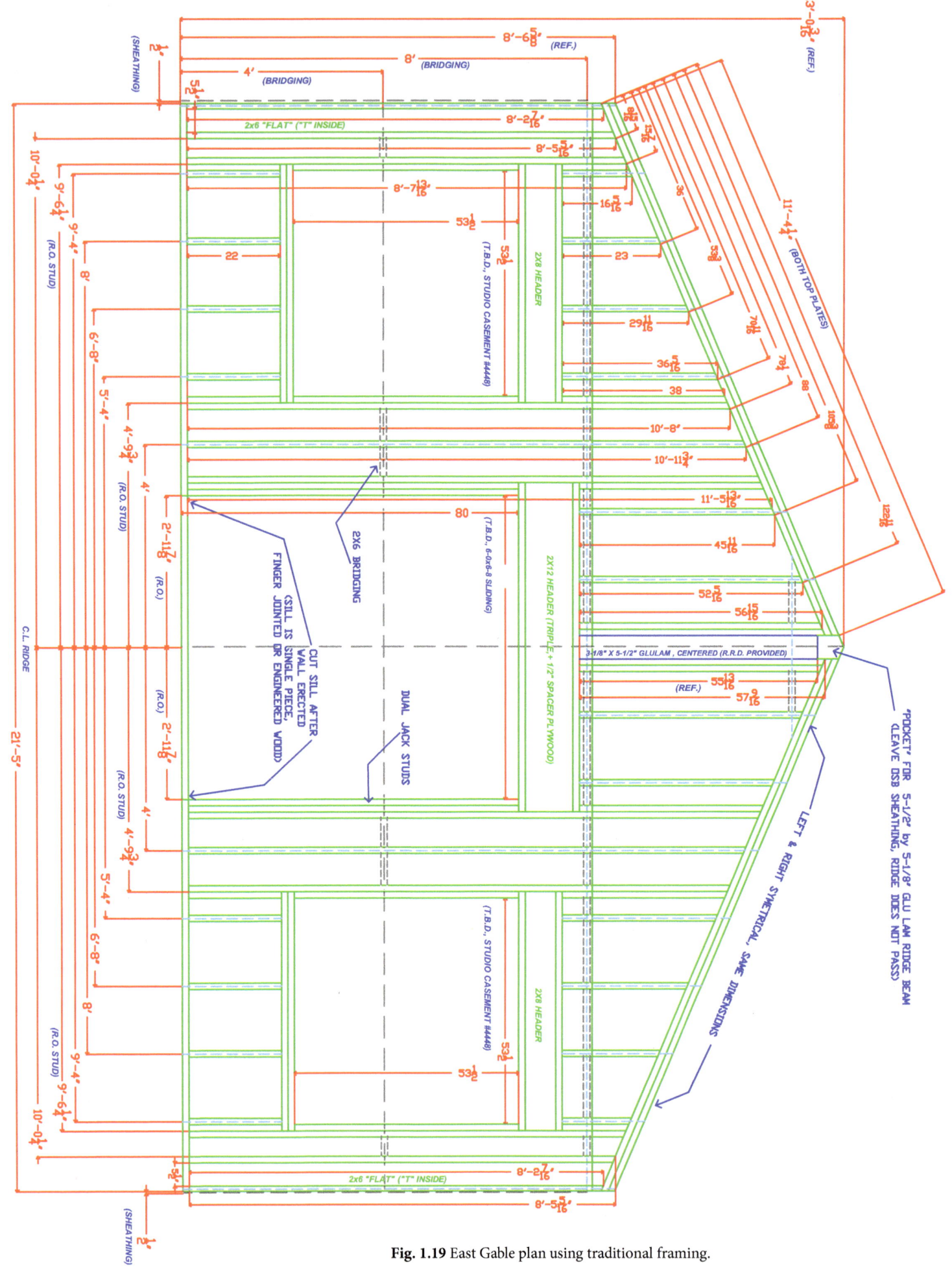

Fig. 1.19 East Gable plan using traditional framing.

STANDARDIZATION (MODULARITY)

Now that the reader has a good idea as to this project's finished look, and the larger SIP conceptual approach, we will show you another example of why we need more standardization, or modularity, in the residential construction industry. The guest house (Fig. 1.17), despite the owner's sincere attempt to utilize SIPs, was actually conventionally stud-framed and used a high-quality spray foam insulation in the framed cavity. The photos you just viewed represent the typical situation a homeowner finds themselves in as they are considering a home purchase. In other words, the photos show only the nice surface and belie the underlying quality of the structure. Figure 1.19 is the actual provided detailed drawing of the East Gable end of the Guest house.

Any framing crew, and I believe many designers and architects, will confirm that this level of framing detail is rarely given to the carpenters. I am telling these carpenters exactly how long, the exact pitch angle, and the location of every stud in this gable-end module. They do not have to, guess, estimate, or attempt any other approach other then to build exactly to the drawing. This is similar to the large 12/12-pitched Mountain Chalet gable shown in Fig. 1.8 east gable plan using traditional framing.

My detailed drawings for this level of construction is done for two reasons: First, they are "standardized" to the fixed Timber Trusses used in my company's system and rarely change once established. (Like a manufactured product.) And second, since I want them to match our Timber Truss profiles consistently in the field, we provide this level of detail.

Using one of my automotive analogies to demonstrate this modularity idea, think of a car you have owned and one of the tire/wheel combinations is destroyed by some freak accident, like brushing a concrete curb. One would expect a remedy is to simply go down to that respective dealer's parts department and buying, maybe financially painful, a new tire/wheel set and installing it on the car. Presto, we are quickly back in business, albeit with a somewhat lighter wallet. The Figure 1.19 framed module can similarly be exchanged with the earlier presented SIP version in Figure 1.15. We could actually "swap out" these two different wall modules, just like big tires, if we really wanted to play with a huge wooden erector set toy. Not sure that this analogy fits? Figure 1.20 (with R40 insulation, window cut-outs, and electrical boxes installed), shows the triple-paneled gable-end SIP section being lifted into place, and demonstrates how SIP construction can make a home construction quick, efficient and very precise.

Fig. 1.20 Large SIP gable-end being lifted.

SIP VS. TRADITIONAL

This 2010 SIP project used the similar 8/12-20' Timber Trusses in the Walnut *EnergyStar* project in Building Today's Green Home (built in 2006). Note the full gable has three sub-sections that were assembled on the floor and lifted by the boom truck to its final location. The bottom line is that this SIP panel version would fit exactly on the earlier 2×6 framed Walnut project; just like the new-wheel analogy. The SIP technology for this project already has the R40 insulation inherent in the SIPs as well as the electrical boxes/conduit runs. Of course the proper rough openings (RO) for the windows are also visible here.

Since the client was convinced that SIPs were too expensive for this Guest House, the contractor (and framing crew) provided cost estimates. So, it was conventionally framed, SIPs were not used. A NHAB builder's monthly newsletter article was also presented to all concerned. The national survey showed the labor for SIP houses was about one-half the cost of conventional stud-framing labor[4].

Want to see just one level of quality the client actually received? Figure 1.21 shows where the premium-grade *Glulam* ridge beam (horizontal 6×6) hits the conventional framed gable end wall. You can see that about one-half of the left 2×6 stud, on the side of the vertical ridge post, is notched away. The result is the approximate 3/4" gap on the right side (note the chainsaw-like "technical adjustment" and gap of light from the outside of the building). I checked each gable after hand-framing before we installed the trusses and noted this almost 1" error in these angled, top plate lengths compared to the dimensions shown in the Fig. 1.19 drawing.

Fig. 1.21 This is just one example of a "custom" project's quality of work. The reality in the residential construction realm is that the underlying work quality is not always good. The 24'-long sides of this house could have been built with just one SIP panel as shown in Fig. 1.13.

Fig. 1.22 An eave 8'×24' SIP being lowered into place.

FLOOR PLANS, MODEST TO MEDIUM

Before we jump into the specifics of each of the floor plan series, I will outline the consistent process that we will utilize to explain each family of plans in each chapter. First, we will begin each plan type with the base floor plan and then show some elevations. Elevations are four views of the house: north, south, east and west. We chose the floor plan first, because, unlike a typical U.S. home-selection process, we are stressing function over form.

We also choose the south elevation as the preferred major window wall, especially if we pre-determined our building lot for passive solar sun usage (and also for some standardization of floor plan patterns). The basic space needs, such as the general size (total sq.ft.) and bedroom/bathroom sizing are addressed first, then the exterior appearances. After going through many of the series types, a distinct pattern of functionality will be apparent. In each chapter, we will present one or two extra add-on elements: entry porches or attached garages, which will show ways to gain both customization and the impact of various terrains on the home sites.

After the floor plan and elevations are shown, we will submit a brief overview of the floor plan and why major elements, like public and private areas are located where they are. A more detailed feature list, a bulleted outline of each room, will follow. Finally, we will show how several steps, when implemented for most designs, can enhance the home to be even more passive-solar oriented. This exercise will also indicate where some homes cannot easily implement passive-solar gain in a generic subdivision setting because of the base requirement that the major window wall face generally south. On average, only one out of four lots are likely to be the most optimum for maximizing passive solar usage. Some of the other percentage of homes can obtain a measure of passive solar gain for specific rooms or add-on features: for example, sunrooms. The serious reader, who is thinking about building a more energy-efficient future home, will do due diligence in selecting their homesite accordingly.

SHOWING USABLE SPACE

As the series plans evolve and move upward in size and complexity, we will indicate areas of the home that are wheelchair friendly. A wheelchair circle should be four feet in diameter. Typically, in tighter zones, like the guest bathroom, a true scale of the space needed for wheelchair access will become clear. We use 36"-wide (3'-0") doors, when it is practical, for the main rooms. The minimum 18" space around the door knob is also important for wheelchair usage, but is difficult to achieve in the smaller-house plans. Since there are a growing number of baby boomers with aging parents, the "feature" column in the Fig. 1.3 matrix will aid in selecting relevant plans. Our goal is to make the home as wheel-chair friendly as possible, but not perfectly ADA compliant.

We show how furniture will fit in the floor plans by using labels calling out beds, cabinets, tables, etc. When choosing one of the smaller 2 bed/2 bath-plans at, say, 1,200 sq.ft., and you plan to put a king-size bed in the smaller guest room, you won't be able to do it. Be realistic. Is the closet sized for this reality also? For example, do I now expect my occasionally-visiting daughter to have a huge closet in our new downsized home?

Another example would be selecting a modest plan with a smaller, yet workable dining room, but wanting to put a huge, possibly a family heirloom, 42"×8' dining table there. One has to think over their most important priorities and then go down that path. Not every path is available if you don't want to own a McMansion! My point is, I've seen many house-plan books and discussed many plans chosen by clients; with trouble lurking. They selected the plan for visual appeal. When I delve into room specifics, the clients typically have no feel for the actual size of specific rooms or how the furniture will fit in those rooms. I also see the pattern of more complex floor plans, with extra halls, angled or disruptive features that remove space where really needed. Again, the furniture will not fit in the rooms because the planned space was simply chopped up and frittered away. The display of actual-size, key furniture pieces is significant in making an effective, overall floor plan decision that works for you.

One compounding factor of furniture placement is in the great room. This room is important to any family, but, it has several factors that make it difficult to design: Window and door placement, walk zones, television placement for viewing, and fireplace (or stove) location.

These factors are generally interrelated to each other and will require some tough choices by the client. You simply cannot have all of them and the desired furniture in one area. For example, a window and a door are not the same thing. Sounds simple, right? Many people select exterior French doors (dual) because they look good in a magazine or plan book. They then move the furniture in and realize they have to provide a walk zone to this door. The 6' for the doors is removed from, say, a 20'-wide major wall, leaving them only 14' for a fireplace, the large LCD/plasma television screen, more windows for light and air, and seating that will tie this all together in some functional manner.

A recent consulting project with a client's great room will demonstrate this dilemma. The client asked me to guide them in the final planning and refining of a chosen floor plan for their weekend home. The great room was about 17'-wide and was adjacent to the bar/counter of the kitchen on one side. The side wall was 90° from the bar/counter and contained the fireplace and two doors to an adjoining sunroom. On the far end of this fireplace wall, and open to the great room, was the dining area. That meant that the fireplace, at about 5'-wide, and the two sets of symmetrical doors on ether side of the fireplace, consumed almost all of the 17' wall space. The door space adjacent to the bar/counter was also where the bar chairs were located. Essentially, the counter seating would be in the walk zone to pass through the door into the sunroom. The second symmetrical door on the other side of the centrally-located fireplace would imply another walk zone. If you drew a couch and living room chair to their properly scaled sizes, they would simply not fit! You could not have two separate doors, two walk zones and furniture in this space. It looked good but it's impossible to make it work. Two key changes aided this client in making the space work: The right-sided door wall was removed and a built-in bookcase/television entertainment zone was located there and the door near the kitchen bar/counter was converted to a cased opening (no door and no swing space needed). The client could then use furniture in a L-shaped arrangement around both the fireplace and the television/entertainment cabinet. And yes, the necessary, but not discussed, windows on the third wall came into useful play. The alleged, original symmetry would have killed the day-to-day utilization of this room. Thus: **Less can be more**. So, displaying some practical furniture layouts is a guide in the right direction.

THIS BOOK CONTAINS PRACTICAL FLOOR PLANS

Our major goal is not just example floor plans, but a methodology of aiding the serious reader in intelligently choosing a home that will address the future U.S. reality. If you are serious, hang on for our journey of utilizing SIPs to get there.

For those readers who don't want to wade through all the different plan types initially, simply spend some time on the feature combinations of the matrix in Fig. 1.3 first. Then, pick out one or two plans that are sized close to your key functional issues. Study the relevant chapter for details to see if your initially-selected floor plan will fit your needs. As a sanity check, pick a second plan from the matrix chart, look over its details and compare to your first selection. For example, a family with an aging parent living full-time in their house, likely with a wheelchair, might want a third bedroom (or den). The total square footage needs would be approaching 2,000 sq.ft., so they could begin their search with either the Winged Chalet #2 or the Squashed H.

Note that the floor dimensions shown are to the inside of the framing, rounded off to the nearest inch. The square-footage numbers for the entire house are the full, outside dimensions. For individual room areas, the dimensions are measured from the outside of an outer wall to the middle of an inner wall or wall center to wall center as applicable. The net area per room will always be less than stated in the text. This gives us a standard that accounts for all the space.

So let's explore a basic home style next.

chapter two

Starting Point: The Basic Chalet

The chalet house shape is almost like apple pie, quite American now, despite its European roots. In New England, this nearly identical twin house is called a Cape (as in the, place south of Boston, where Puritan travelers landed some time back). This quite simple geometric shape, generally considered spatially efficient, is the root of its beauty and also the clue to key limitations. Essentially it approaches a conceptual cube, with the steeper roof, typically a 12/12 pitch, which adds to this cubical effect. The steeper pitch enables what is really a 1-1/2 story house, not a full two-story design. Out of the New England region we typically see this shape in mountain, lake, or vacation regions. Its value is due to this compactness, particularly for weekender situations. Its smaller footprint is important for smaller building lots. However, this weekender use indicates why it is <u>only our beginning</u>. We will then migrate these many floor plan series forward to versions that achieve a more flexible living style. However, the two variations we cover here, will amplify this evolution process, yet still will have value for some homeowners.

Huge 12/12 pitch gable end wall top section being placed.

Fig. 2.1 The most basic chalet is #18A, at just over 1,600 sq.ft. in a two bedroom, 2-1/2 bath configuration. Figure 2.1 displays the basic main floor plan while Figure 2.2 is the loft or half upper level plan. The key wording here is both the half bath and the half level. As noted in *Today's GREEN Home*, about the less/more concept, the extra half bath, generally thought in modern terms as the powder room, is a direct result of the efficiency, or conversely observed, the smallness, of the footprint. As noted, this extra half bath generally is requested by clients since the master bedroom, preferred on the main level, usually has this bedroom as private. That is, one most go through the master bedroom door to find this only bathroom on the main level. Thus, visiting guests have the powder room (and the extra cost it bears).

Fig. 2.1 shows that this plan is almost the traditional version of what most of us think as the weekend cabin. The public area, the living, kitchen, and dining zones are clustered in an open great room area with the private bedroom on the other end of the footprint. The line of demarcation, for efficiency, is the almost centered stairs. This staircase position carries over to the loft and basement level and provides a clue to its limitations beyond the weekend use. A Queen truss is used to support the open roof structure. (Queen is our generalization of the style with the extra two angle webs coming out from the traditional king post in the center of the truss.)

STARTING POINT: THE BASIC CHALET   27

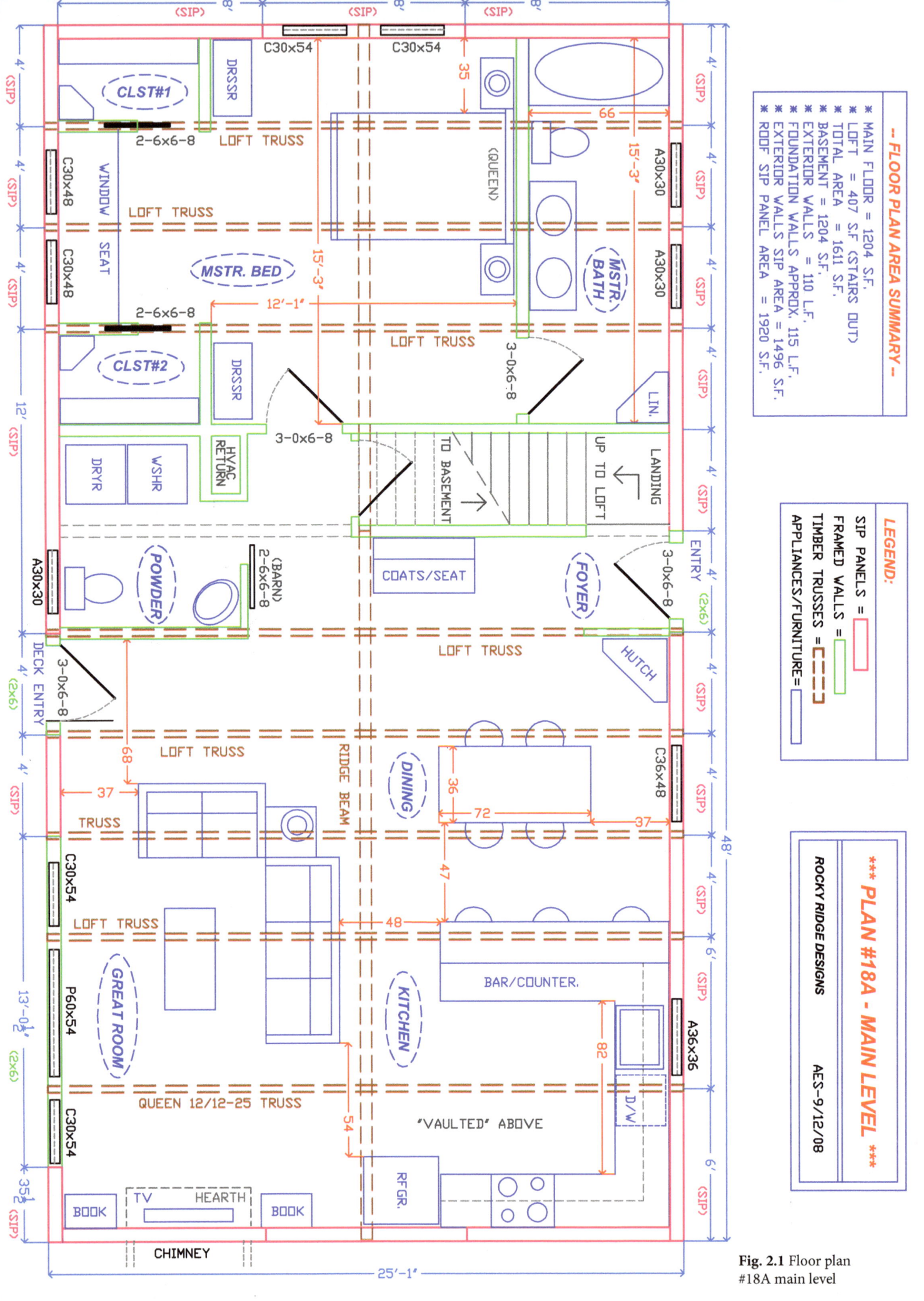

Fig. 2.1 Floor plan #18A main level

MAIN FLOOR ROOM SPECIFICS OF CHALET

18A Great Room Highlights

- About 282 sq.ft. in a rectangular 12'- deep by 23'- 5"- wide zone
- Long 23'- 5"-wide wall enables 3-window combination, plus door
- Gable end, side wall allows fireplace near corner with flanking bookcases.
- Note: chimney not at low-maintenance preferred high point of gable end.
- Area over fireplace goes to full 12/12 roof height (with Queen Truss)
- Open to and adjacent to both kitchen and dining areas

18A Dining Room Highlights

- About 144 sq.ft. in rectangular 12'-deep by 12'-wide zone
- Single wall zone allows one window centered under trusses
- Open to kitchen and Great Room is efficient for minimizing hall/walkways
- Short wall near entry door enables "budget" foyer and corner zone for hutch

18A Master Bathroom

- Almost 90 sq.ft. in rectangular 6'-deep by 16'-wide zone (net 5'- 6" width)
- Truss standard width profile still enables slightly oversize (66") tub on end
- Two window potential on long wall
- Very efficient layout, minimal wall framing needed

18A Kitchen Highlights

- About 144 sq.ft. in a rectangular 12'-deep by 12'- wide zone
- Corner placement against gable end provides some cabinet zones
- Enables U-shaped zone with bar-counter adjacent to dining
- Suspended, low profile upper cabinets over bar counter possible immediately adjacent to great room
- Two-wall corner approach enables window and oven vent potential

18A Master Bedroom Highlights

- About 220 sq.ft. in rectangular 12'-deep by 16'-wide zone, plus bump-out (window seat)
- Window seat, dual-closet "nook" opposite bed wall
- Gable end side wall enables larger window placement
- Corner nooks near closets allow dresser placement
- Traffic path through room to closet and bath is effective
- Note: Master bedroom and loft bedroom above share footprint

18A Master Closet Highlights

- Dual (his and her) 4'-deep by 6'-wide zones
- Side doors preserve dresser space in main room
- Window seat enables deep pullout drawers below
- Cathedral ceiling can be obtained by using loft zone above (storage shelves above 8' level)

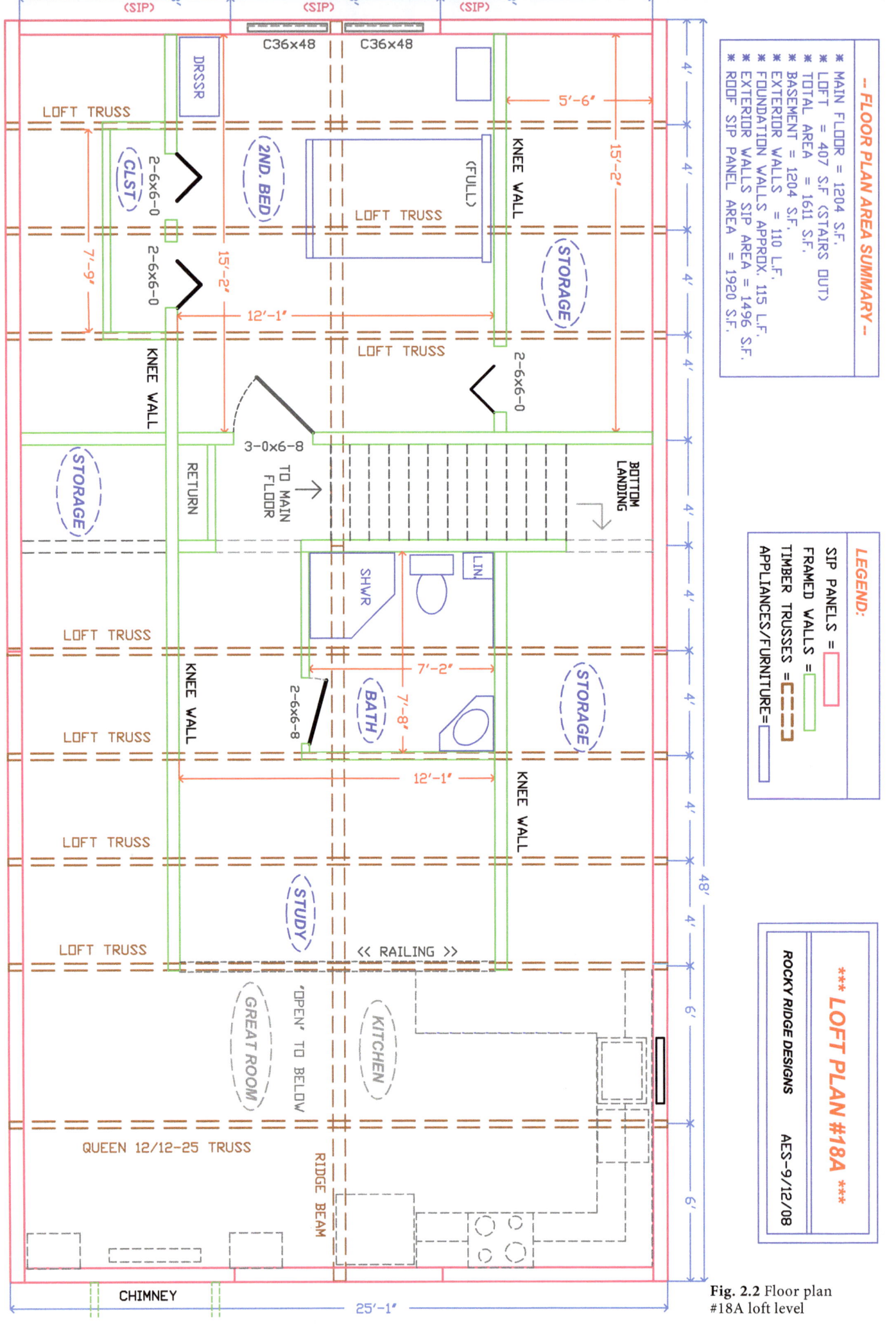

Fig. 2.2 Floor plan #18A loft level

LOFT-LEVEL ROOM SPECIFICS

18A Loft Bedroom Highlights

- About 192 sq.ft. in rectangular 12'-wide by 16'-long zone. Note: directly over master bedroom–privacy limitation)
- Single gable end wall enables two windows
- Can use most of both knee wall zones (about 5' high) for storage
- Cozy loft/nook feeling

18A Loft Bathroom Highlights

- About 60 sq.ft. in rectangular 8'-wide by 7'- 6" zone
- Shower, toilet, and vanity can be squeezed in area (shower must fit near ridge for code headroom minimum)
- Plumbing can fit between Timber trusses (second lower ceiling below over entry foyer area)

18A Loft Closet Highlights

- Can use most of both knee wall zones for storage
- Can do built-in cabinet module opposite bed location (limited by 5' maximum height)

18A Loft Den Highlights

- Extra L-shaped Den zone (about 140 sq.ft.)
- Long knee wall zone good bookcase zone
- Can accommodate small desk/computer work zone
- Open railing end dramatically overlooks Great Room & Queen Truss

Fig. 2.3 (Left) Note that the Timber Truss pattern changes to the wider 6' increment over the great room gable end due to the visual open area to the roof. The private end of the structure has the closer 4' spacing to support the second floor structure (loft).

Fig. 2.4 (Below) The floor of the loft provides an attractive wood beamed ceiling, but flat, in the main levels below the loft ceiling. The contrast in height of the loft ceiling (left zone-over the kitchen bar area) and the vaulted open area in the adjacent dining area (on right-where roof supporting Queen truss is located) is more evident here. This roof/ceiling contrast, of course, is to gain the ceiling headroom so the upper loft area is useful.

Fig. 2.5 (Facing page) To provide an overview of the structure, and some dimensions for reference, a section, or slice, of this cabin design is shown in Figure 2.5. (Assumed here as slab foundation, but highlighting the important loft zone dimensions). The tall 12/12 pitched trusses are required to obtain enough usable head room in the loft second floor area without adding a full story. (Not adding large dormers on one side, as typical in the cape version). The very tall center of this loft area is metered against the 5' side, or knee wall height. This results in about a 12' room width, or something less than 50% of the building's 25' total footprint width (actually 48% here). Also, the 25' span is about the minimum width to actually get the staircase in and still have a typical code-minimum 36"-wide hall zone at the loft floor. In fact, we need the landing at the bottom as the first step/riser. Yet, like the New England Cape Cottage, it still provides some maximizing of footprint size via this vertical increase.

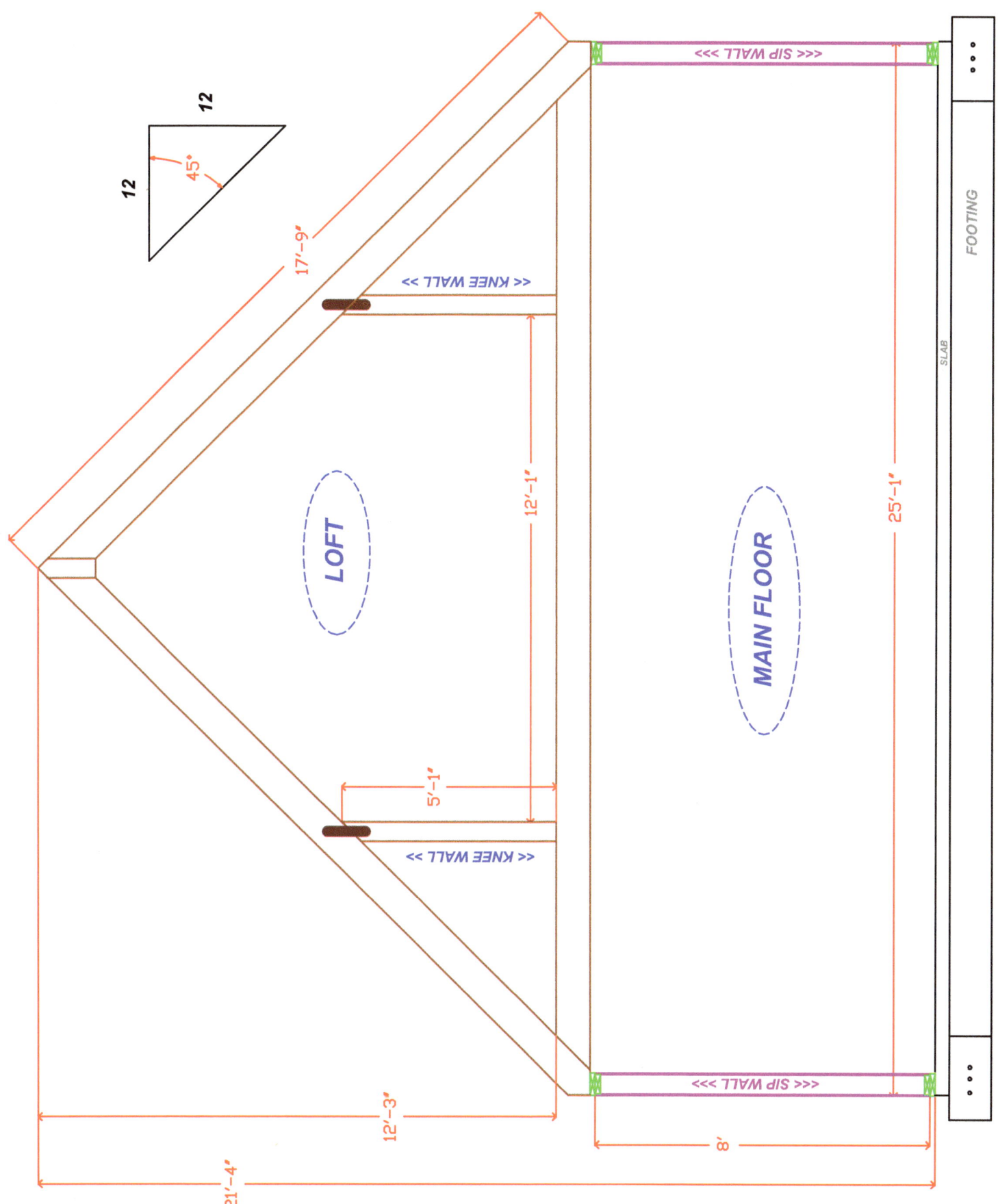

Fig. 2.5 Section view of #18A (with loft).

Fig. 2.6 This photo of the knee walls on the loft sides will aid in understanding the physical limits there. Essentially, this 5'-side is the practical limit of usefulness. In fact, most real estate appraisers will not count the extra floor area as valid if these walls are less than 5' high (Even I will bump my head here!).

LIMITATIONS OF CHALET LOFT LEVEL

As we move on to the second or loft level in this Chalet 18A series, we will see some limitations of this traditional shape. Some of the limitations of the chalet profile may now be evident. However, an exercise in optimizing this base foot print even more is shown if we examine the "larger" 18B Plan.

One can quickly observe that there is little difference in the Main floors of both 18A and 18B, particularly since the footprint is identical (48 ft. by 25 ft.) However, the subtle points we will show here in 18B set the ground work for all of the Cathedral Ranch family of plans. First the only difference on the main floor is around the staircase (now no basement). Note that the door under the stairs is now a coat closet with an access door behind the closet. The space behind the closet enables a zone to locate the hot water heater and keep it on the preferred main floor location (since we are on a slab foundation, no basement). This also removes one of the main mechanical needs for the house, with the balance of the HVAC (heating, ventilation, air conditioning) going upstairs. Note also the significance of the larger HVAC chute near the powder room. It alleviates some of the pressure of not having a basement coupled with an exposed beam (Timber Truss) for running some of the ducting.

But the real structural issue now is that the entire first floor uses the loft-style truss completely. Thus, we have giving up the more glamorous open cathedral roof when we use the Queen Truss as in Plan 18A to gain more space in the loft. By the way, remember that due to the very tall 12/12 Chalet style roof profile, this cathedral, or vaulted ceiling is about 22' above the main level, but only 13' above the loft level. Thus, we are going for the more practical issue of gaining space and giving up something cosmetically, particularly since we don't have the luxury of the basement expansion space. Thus, we have the flat, yet, still beamed T&G decked ceiling throughout the main floor. Let's see what is now happening in the increased loft space.

UTILIZING ALL THE SPACE

Since the small triangle zones behind the loft knee walls are almost completely the length of the building, we can use this for the HVAC mechanicals. We would utilize a horizontal air handler, preferably a heat-pump system, and lay out the main HVAC plenums on this floor (which is now the wood-decked ceiling for the main level). We can also run some of the plenums on the opposite side and feed across the building in the false ceiling zone under the loft bedroom plumbing and over the entry foyer. (Basically the ceiling here on the main floor is at the bottom of the truss collar beam, not at the top like the balance of the main floor.) Note that the line up of the knee walls with the loft's larger bedroom with the master bedroom below, as well as through the den and third bedroom also, facilitates plumbing and wiring runs in this timber beam structure.

The utilization (full house length) of these outboard triangular wings in the larger 18B plan is a crucial element in the significant enhancement over plan 18A. Essentially, we now have fully taken advantage of the chalet's structural shape (without adding dormers, etc. that is typically employed, along with the cost and other issues).

Since this third bedroom is the key difference in the loft zone, we will only detail this room. Also, the elevation views of 18B are so similar to 18A, we won't display them here. And because our focus in this work is more on the evolution of plans <u>beyond the chalet shape</u>, we won't detail an example SIP wall module as included in the following chapters' plans.

CHALET'S LIMITATIONS LEAD TO CATHEDRAL RANCH CONCEPT

The second half of the two major chalet steep-roof-pitch issues involves the comfort sense of the loft zone. The nook feeling up there is partially due to the vaulted, (cathedral ceiling) coupled with its realistic size. Specifically, even the net 13'-high peak in the middle, at the ridge beam, and the shorter 5' knee walls invoke a cozy zone (particularly for kids). It is

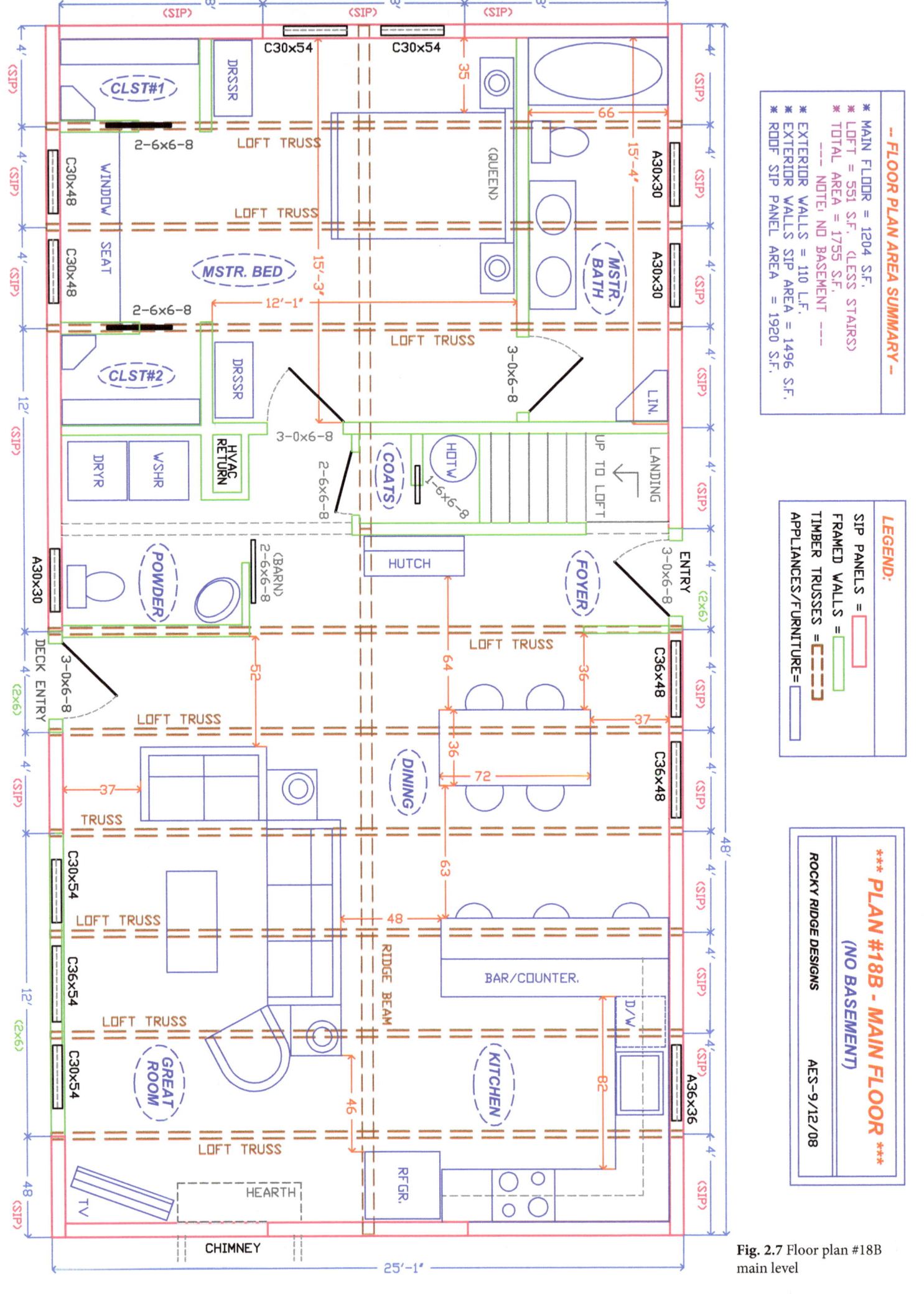

Fig. 2.7 Floor plan #18B main level

not the extreme warehouse-like feel of, quite frankly, an overly tall room. Compare the actual effect of being in the full two-story open cathedral zone (22' tall) in the great room in plan 18A (on the main level floor). In this narrow 12'-wide first floor zone with the Queen Truss in the middle, is, at first, striking. Over time, some people will begin to sense that this space is too vertical in look and feel; what I refer to as the "elevator shaft" effect. This pattern is easily detected in many of the United States' McMansions or somewhat slightly less in starter castles entry foyers. This over-ostentation focus on size-over-quality really manifests itself here.

I must inject a little of my cynicism at this point to aid the reader in gauging the relativeness of the chalet shape. This short term meanness is truly intended as a visualizing tool only. Factor in that this cubical shape frequently is a necessity at older, developed, more congested building areas (near-city older suburbs found in New England, New York, etc.) due to the smaller building lot sizes and/or, of course, simply higher land costs. But our goal here is to aid those readers actively seeking a smarter solution for their future home. Thus, I frequently used the acronym YANC (Yet Another Nothing Chalet), Yes, it sounds like what the British used to call us Americans in describing the explosion of mountain cabins I was seeing over-built in the north Georgia Mountains in the late 1990s on until about 2006. (Also in North Carolina, Tennessee, South Carolina, etc.) Just consider that this phenomenon eerily paralleled the McMansion boom in America. But, these homes were generally intended as weekender second homes, but, a surprising number actually became retirement homes (Hmm?).

The point here is to suggest that there may be a better floor plan concept, if the client can and wants to make that choice.

Yet, despite this initially negative label, a comfortable weekender-like cabin typically appeared is shown in Fig. 2.7. But, we want to move on <u>beyond</u> this "cubical" shaped house. Many of the technical points exposed here will be expanded in the following chapters.

LOFT-LEVEL ROOM SPECIFICS

Plan #18B overview

- An extra 144 sq.ft., but the result is significant, being based on the same 48'-long by 25'-wide footprint as noted in Figure 2.8 and Figure 2.9
- Think of 18B in tight neighborhood zones where the lot size dictates this two-story reality
- Does not have a basement. (For this example there could have been basement on right lot)

Loft Level Room specifics of plan 18B

- Loft area available to 576 sq.ft. Thus, a net increase of 144 sq.ft.
- Nets a respectable third bedroom of approximately 12' by 12'
- Limitations due to the 5' knee-wall height on the long sides and the smaller bathroom
- Retained the den area with the third bedroom gain
- Note that a skylight addition in the wall-locked den becomes significant

18B Loft Third Bedroom Highlights

- About 144 sq.ft., 12'-wide by 12'-long zone
- Single gable end wall enables two windows
- Knee-wall zones (about 5' high) can be used for storage/closet
- Cozy loft/nook feeling (see Fig. 2.6)

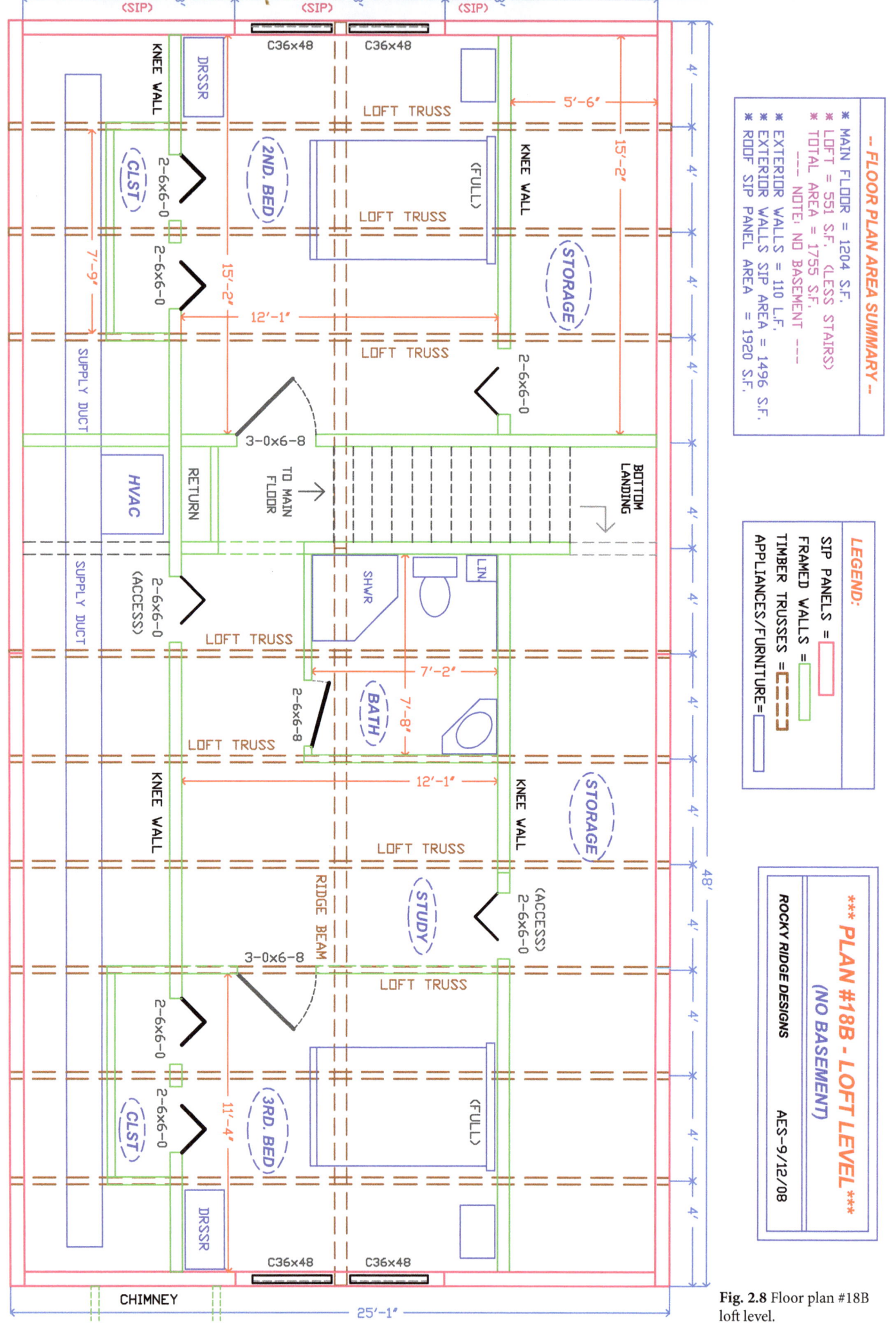

Fig. 2.8 Floor plan #18B loft level.

Fig. 2.9 The zone behind the loft knee walls.

Sufficient for now, this is just a signal to alert our rational thinking to weigh in with the emotional appearance factors when one first sees these chalets. Like: "Wow, look at the steep vaulted ceiling and that neat loft".

But, I will inject one more factor to weigh as we delve into these different floor plan styles/shapes: Roof factor, both gross and net. Essentially, these roof-factor figures are verifying that the cubical chalet shape appears to be gaining much floor space per roof area. But there is more traded off in the chalet.

The key observation should be that the neater, more dramatic ceiling, or warmer zone, is in the loft, or second floor, not on the main floor level. The parallel penalty is that the main floor has the flatter, more compromised roof under those loft zones. Factor in that the typical suburban construction would likely be a cost-reduced *Sheetrock* ceiling and not the warmer/stronger wood-&-beamed examples displayed here. (Please, don't anyone bring up tray ceiling here, done in *Sheetrock*; no real quality, won't even touch the look and feel of Fig. 2.4, not even close!)

Thus, living <u>principally on the main floor is</u> a key design goal for retiring baby boomers. How can we capture the feel of the loft cathedral roof, but do it on the main level and without the physical penalties of the second floor structure? Simple! We just eliminate the second floor entirely! Onward to progress.

STARTING POINT: THE BASIC CHALET 39

chapter three

Modularity – What & Why ?

So, what is modularity and why is it so important to understanding the home floor plans to follow? Here is my outline of this approach:
- Reusing proven sub-assemblies (modules) to improve the home's quality, construction time, and cost
- Modules can range from individual physical parts to full assemblies (small, medium, or large) and also to proven methods
- But continue using only if they are still effective (these can be updated or revised)

Generally, even in the residential construction industry, improvement in the final end product, homes, is frequently marked by some level of modularity, but is not usually identified as such. For example, one of the most fundamental and significant early technology jumps is the epitome of modules: The standardized 2×4, 2×6, etc. framing lumber. Contrast these consistently sized, mass produced, lower cost, wood pieces to early framing techniques. Before that, the builder literally had to start with the trees on the stump or at best, ones already felled and then only a rough-sawn block with a multitude of shapes and sizes to deal with. Then, many more steps and processes to obtain usable components. Even the relatively modern full Timber-Framing process requires a lot of steps to get usable beam sizes. This a key factor of the higher priced traditional timber framed homes.

With this basic 2×4 module example, we can move on to more significant sized module types that really multiply our efficiency and effectiveness. The key medium-sized modules we will utilize here:

- Exterior wall SIPs, typically 64" wide by 8' tall
- Timber Trusses, low-cost standard-sized pine beams, 5/12 roof pitch and 20' long
- Interior gable-end framing that matches the profile shape of 2×6-framed Timber Trusses
- Matching exterior 20'-long gable-end SIPs
- Small window version of 64" exterior SIP that can be reused in multiple rooms
- Insulating EPS foam panels, typically 4'×8' for ceiling "sandwich" technique
- 2×8 t&g pine decking for exposed ceiling on the interior of the home
- Spray foam the exterior framed walls for non-SIP zones, i.e., above the top plate truss heel height

We can also use multiple sets of these medium sized modules to create larger units. A couple examples you will see later in the floor plans:

- 4-5 truss set in the great room, 32' long or 26'-8" long, all are 20' wide
- Two-truss master bedroom, 16' × 20'
- One-truss smaller bedroom, 10'-8" × 20'
- Master bath/master closet is standard layout for the smaller, more compact house plans

Let's expand on the details behind the medium module set and why their use leads to more effective home construction. In Chapter 1 we have shown the details of the many levels of SIP wall construction on a system level. The individual module specifics here are important.

SIP EXTERIOR WALLS

Typically only 64" wide and only 8' tall to match Timber Truss and gable wall spans

- A two man crew can lift and install these panels that are about 130-140 pounds; no boom truck is needed for these smaller panels
- 4×6, S4S (all four sides are finished), pine-posts measuring 3-1/2" × 5-1/2" at junctions to support Timber Trusses
- Junction pine posts can be from same supplier as Timber Truss beams
- Mid-wall panels, supporting the trusses, have 1-3/4"-deep × 5-1/2"-wide vertical foam recesses at junctions for 4×6 post insert
- End-wall panels have a typical 1-1/2"-deep recess for 2×6 vertical end wall plates or for joining to an adjacent 2×6 pre-framed module, i.e., a multiple window section
- An inner bottom 2×6 plate and an inner top 2×6 plate fit into the horizontal 1-1/2" × 5-1/2" foam recesses
- Since the plans utilize simple slab foundations, we use a pressure-treated extra 2×8 sill plate ripped to 6-1/2" wide right on the slab, under the SIP and the inner bottom plate
- By adding an extra 2×8 sill plate ripped to 6-1/2" wide at the top, we have doubled the strength of the wall, which is now 8'-3" high
- By repeating the panel-and-post installation sequence, putting up the walls is fairly rapid, including caulking, proper nailing, etc.
- Zones with gable-wall framing without Timber Truss support can use longer SIPs, which may need a boom truck to lift them, and not require the 4×6 post when this longer panel passes an internal wall. The typical SIP fasteners are used at these junctions
- Finished panels are factory built, which means each panel is exactly the same. Panels built on site can lead to inconsistently constructed panels
- Insulation is typically R22 with EPS foam, which is already installed as part of panel[5]
- Using the details in shop drawings, electrical chases, horizontal and vertical, can be cut into the SIPs at the factory
- Standardized, medium, single-window SIPs can be used in multiples in construction

SIP PANEL NOTES : (VIEWED FROM OUTSIDE)

1- ALL WALL SIP PANELS ARE 6-1/2" THICK (5-1/2" EPS FOAM, R22)
2- TOP & BOTTOM HORIZONTAL FOAM "RELIEFS" ARE 1-1/2" DEEP (FOR 2X6)
3- WALL "END" VERTICAL FOAM "RELIEFS" ARE 1-1/2" DEEP (FOR 2X6)
4- EAVE, MID-WALL, @ TRUSSES, VERTICAL FOAM "RELIEFS" ARE 1-3/4" DEEP (FOR 4x6 POST)
5- 'GABLE-END', PANELS ARE JUMBO, RUNNING VERTICAL
6- "GABLE" PANELS, END WALL FOAM RELIEFS ARE 1-1/2" DEEP (FOR 2x6)
7- "GABLE" PANEL MID-WALL FOAM RELIEFS ARE 1-3/4" DEEP (FOR 4x6 POST)
8- ELECTRICAL BOXES & WIRING CHASES AS NOTED (ONE GABLE SET ON LEFT, ONE ON RIGHT)
9- WIRING CHASES IN "EAVE" PANELS ONLY VERTICAL, TO TOP, GABLES ONLY HORIZONTAL
10- WINDOW 2x6 BLOCKING INSTALLED AT FACTORY, ALL OTHER PLATES FIELD INSTALLED/SUPPLIED

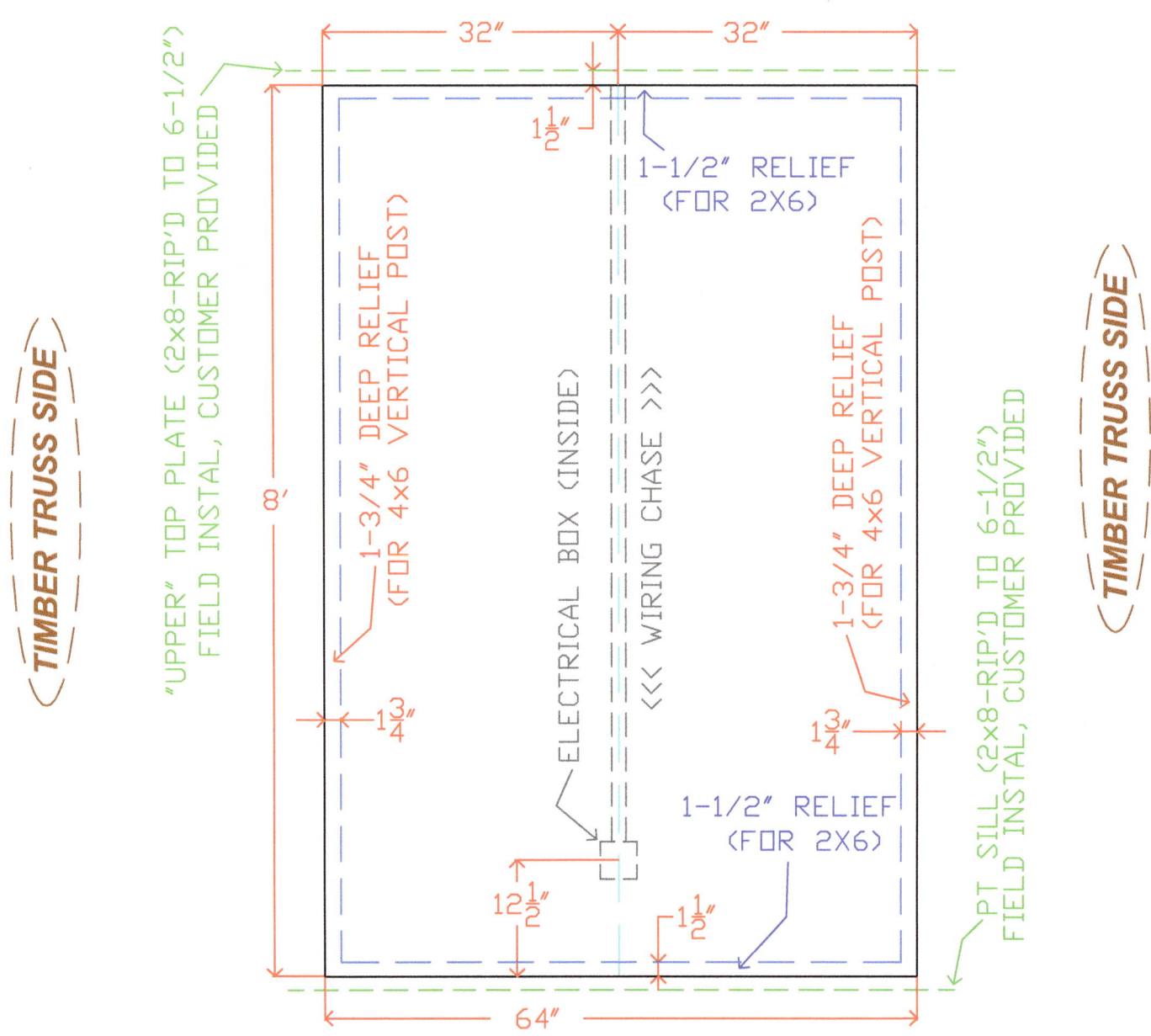

Figure 3.1 – Standard 64"-wide exterior wall SIP
A minor variation of this standard SIP module can have a small 36"× 36" window framed in the center as shown in Figure 3.2. In some of the following floor plans, this windowed SIP can be used as many as three times; all identical as a module, but still workable in rooms as indicated in the floor plans. Typical spots for this panel is as a bathroom or kitchen window. There is also a version of this windowed panel with larger 42" × 30" window.

SIP PANEL NOTES : (VIEWED FROM OUTSIDE)

1- ALL WALL SIP PANELS ARE 6-1/2" THICK (5-1/2" EPS FOAM, R22)
2- TOP & BOTTOM HORIZONTAL FOAM "RELIEFS" ARE 1-1/2" DEEP (FOR 2X6)
3- WALL "END" VERTICAL FOAM "RELIEFS" ARE 1-1/2" DEEP (FOR 2X6)
4- EAVE, MID-WALL, @ TRUSSES, VERTICAL FOAM "RELIEFS" ARE 1-3/4" DEEP (FOR 4X6 POST)
5- 'GABLE-END', PANELS ARE JUMBO, RUNNING VERTICAL
6- "GABLE" PANELS, END WALL FOAM RELIEFS ARE 1-1/2" DEEP (FOR 2X6)
7- "GABLE" PANEL MID-WALL FOAM RELIEFS ARE 1-3/4" DEEP (FOR 4X6 POST)
8- ELECTRICAL BOXES & WIRING CHASES AS NOTED (ONE GABLE SET ON LEFT, ONE ON RIGHT)
9- WIRING CHASES IN "EAVE" PANELS ONLY VERTICAL, TO TOP, GABLES ONLY HORIZONTAL
10- WINDOW 2X6 BLOCKING INSTALLED AT FACTORY, ALL OTHER PLATES FIELD INSTALLED/SUPPLIED

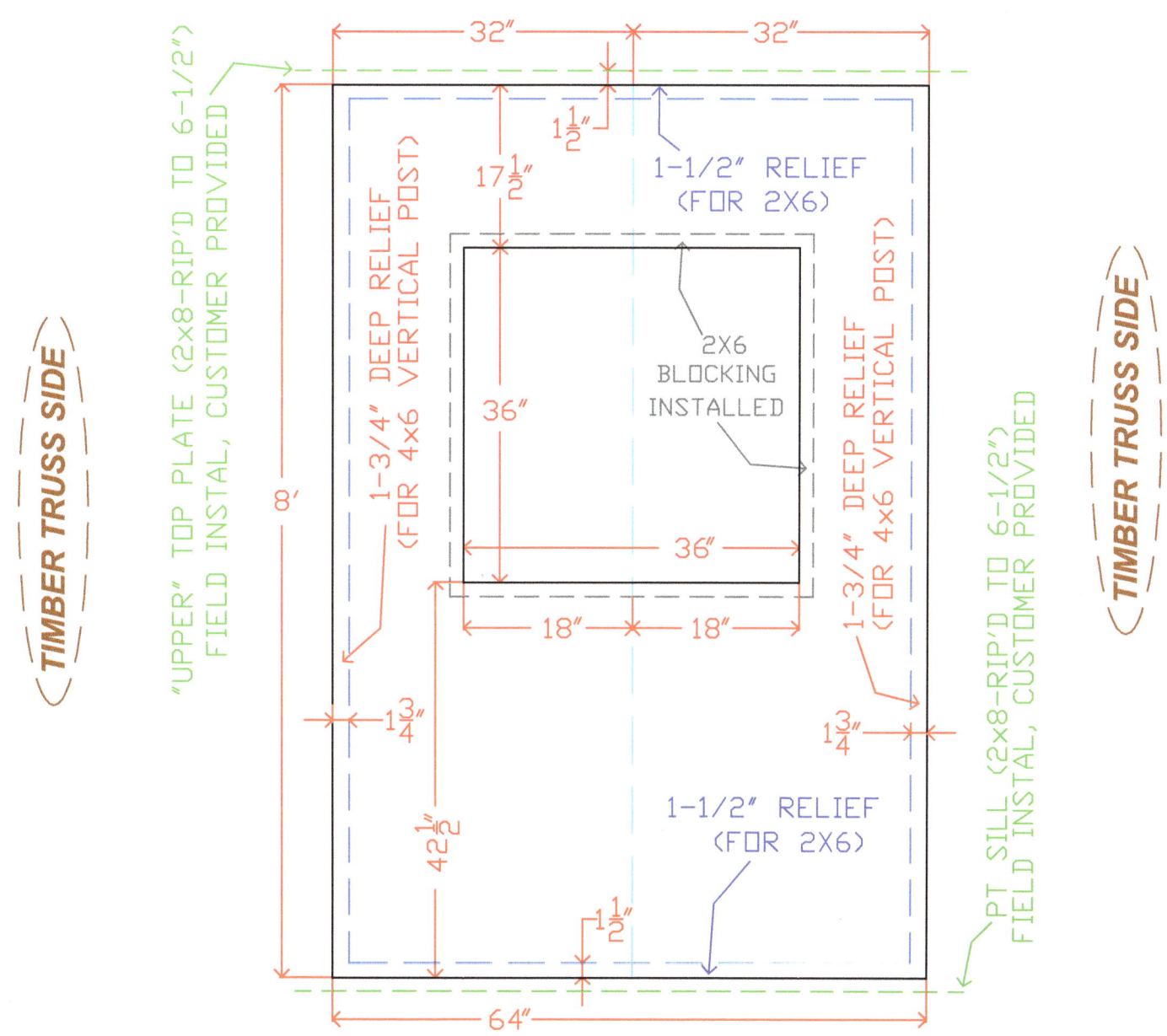

Figure 3.2 – 64"-wide SIP with 36"× 36" window opening. In complex floor plans, a few exterior walls work best if 2×6 framed, spray foamed for insulation, and, if needed, OSB skin sides are added. This 2×6 approach is used in large window sections on the south walls of a passive solar homes. The south walls have many openings due to windows being closer together without much panel width left between them for minimum SIP structure (see fig. 1.6). Using standard 2×6 framing for these sections is more prudent; SIPs don't need to be used everywhere.

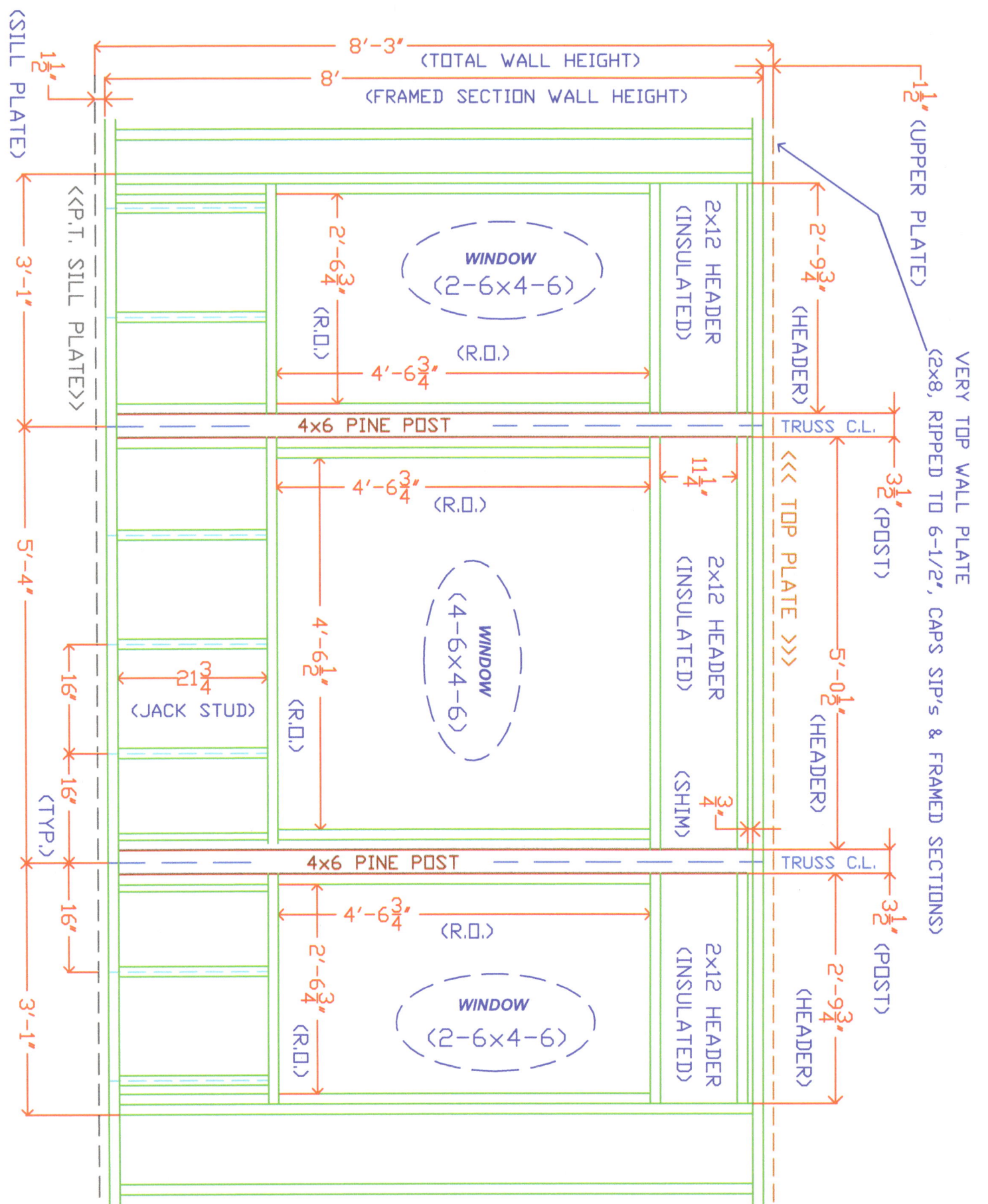

Fig. 3.3 Framed, not SIP, south window wall example.

With the exterior walls installed, we'll show how Timber Trusses hold up the roof.

The Timber Truss approach is not a full timber framing style and is applied to the roof structure components above the typical 8'-high wall. Set on a properly supported wall, Timber Trusses have more point loading at the 64" zones or, where 4×6 posts or triple 2×6 studs are installed.

We prefer Timber Trusses for these kind of homes for several key interrelated factors:
- Typically they can be much stronger than traditionally framed ceilings
- Naturally enables vaulted ceiling while still keeping modest 8'-high primary exterior walls at eaves and 13' at the roof ridge peak
- By using attractive 2×8 pine T&G decking on top of the trusses, we gain natural ceiling beauty plus an incredibly strong roof; 40-50 lb./sq.ft. roof vs. typically framed roof at 20lb./sq.ft.
- Flat foam EPS panels are installed directly on the T&G decking with a final plywood top sheathing is an efficient installation process
- The triple-sandwich of T&G, foam, and top plywood sheathing compounds the structure's strength. Compare this with a typical home that has only 7/16"-thick OSB (oriented strand board) sheathing over 2×4 trusses that are hidden in the attic
- The 64" spacing utilized here makes it possible to have 128"-wide, single-truss second bedroom(s). The 16'-wide, dual-truss room is good for master bedrooms

NON-VENTED VS. VENTED ROOFS

Our Timber Truss vaulted roofs are a non-vented design. Hi-grade EPS foam panels are used in the pitched roof line, not on the flat ceiling. The resulting exposed, vaulted space is utilized, visible, and conditioned as part of the main house HVAC needs.
- Traditional vented roofs are finally getting proper understanding on their flaws, mainly just cheaper. Because this vented attic space has huge temperature swings in the warmer months, i.e., 110-140 degrees F when outside temperatures are in the 80-90 degree range This means your HVAC is working against this abnormally, artificially generated, high temperature in this triangular top zone vs. the actual outdoor temperature. Common sense will tell you that your power bills will follow the real temperature generated there, not optimistic hopes
- Our non-vented version is only working against the outside 80-90 degree range, not the artificial temperature rise in the vented attic. Vented has been the code because it is minimum, cheap, easy, etc.
- The recently trending taller roof pitches, i.e., 8/12-12/12, make it worse with even more hot air volume and more roof structure cost for the larger roof pitch

The Timber Truss features list is of a practical nature, true to our central theme here. But the Timber Truss/vaulted wood beam ceiling has a key emotional value also. Note the typical profile of the customers we are targeting here:
- Clients are typically older, retiring, and are planning for downsizing
- Likely not building in crowded inner-city zones, but likely out to suburbs or rural areas
- Likely have owned the traditionally-framed, flat-ceiling, blah homes of the suburbs
- Are likely interested in a more casual cabin, softer, natural wood like environment

Before delving into the Timber Truss technical points, let's do a quick test of the emotional value of the Timber Truss roof concept. See fig. 1.1, which displays an excess of external trim on typical suburban homes. Fig. 1.2 shows the comfortable Timber Truss interior. Which one would you choose based upon emotional value? Which leads to: "Where do you want to spend your money?"

Some key points in our suggested low-cost Timber Trusses will show the importance of this high value design choice.

Fig. 3.4 Low-cost 5/12-20' pine-beam truss
The finalized version of this truss is a heavier version, a 6 ×12 rafter, used for a larger project.

TIMBER TRUSSES

Simpler, King-style trusses use standard eastern white pine, S4S finish, smooth, not rustic. Beam sizes are 4×12 and 4×6.
- Five beam parts per truss: 2 rafters 4×12-12' long, 2 collars 4×6-18' long, and one King post is 4×12-4' long.
- Roof pitch is a modest, but nice, 5/12 pitch with the ridge almost 13' high and 8'-high eave walls.
- Medium 20' span enables a wide array of floor plans with the same truss used everywhere.
- Beams are made from standard steel tooling plates to facilitate, consistent, and rapid beam layout in the shop.
- Beam connections are made with ¼"-thick steel plates which are laser-cut and have a black, powder-coated finish. These plates are installed using 5/8", grade 5 bolts.
- Steel plate parts are only 3 types, total of 12 parts, and include the base wall mounting brackets, which aid in quick installation on wall top.
- 5/8"-diameter grade 5 bolts means that all 14, ¾" holes can be drilled in the beams at the shop.
- Beam shop-fabrication time is about 1-1/2 hours per truss
- The 6×6 ridge beam, slightly modified with the 5/12 roof pitch angle on the top corners, can be supplied by the beam/post supplier. A tooled plate, to indicate the profile cut, is used by our local beam guy to make quickly in shop.
- The final Timber Truss assembly time at the site is typically 30-40 minutes each. Traditional hand-fabrication on site can take hours per beam part.
- Low-cost, black plastic caps cover both bolt heads and nuts to match the black, powder-coated steel plates.

Before moving on to the next module, some price estimates on this simple King truss will be quite useful in gauging their effectiveness. First we should start with two cost references. My earlier truss shop business, Rocky Ridge Designs, produced a full house group of Timber Trusses for around $1200-$1500 each, usually 6-9 trusses. That system used special socket head hardware to disguise bolt heads with matching powder coat, high-grade southern yellow pine *Glulam* beams that were special ordered and were twice as strong as natural pine beams. More sophisticated truss

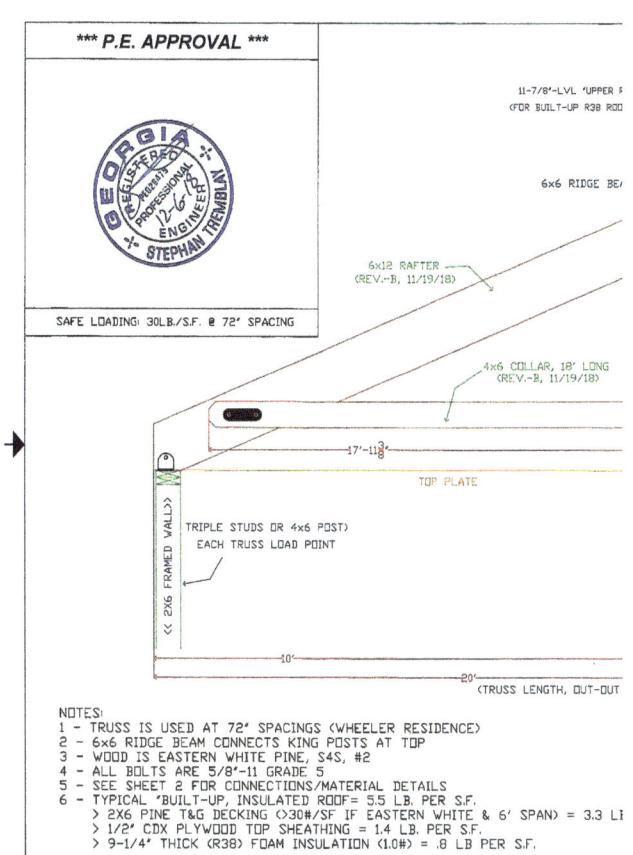

FIGURE 3.5 Timber Truss PE sign off drawing

shapes, i.e., Queen style, use more beam parts, angled webs, plates, and typically longer spans of 24-26'. For reference, the reader can reference my earlier work, Building Today's Green Home, by Art Smith, for the more complex, yet very attractive, 8/12-20' Queen trusses used in the great room of the *EnergyStar* rated home discussed there. See chapter one fig. 1.2.

By observing many other fully hand-built trusses and also many drafting/consulting projects for another Timber Truss framing shop, I saw prices of $2,000 - $3,000 per truss range.

LOW-COST TIMBER TRUSSES

The larger, 6' span, 6×12 Timber Trusses used in the projects shown here ranged about $900-$1000 each, including the truss kit costs. The 64" spacing version with 4'×12' used in these plans cost about $600-$700 each.

It is important to compare the Timber Truss costs to the floor plan by area cost to understand the value of this approach vs. the cost of standard constructed roofs. Let's start with typical home construction engineered trusses made with 2×4s, many small web parts, and thin, pound-in, metal plates. My projects have shown those to run around $2.50 to $3.00 per square foot in 2019 prices. These are typically on 2' centers. This style is not cosmetically intended for vaulted ceilings. The dramatic effect of using the vaulted ceiling zone is shown in all the upcoming floor plans.

Using the same approximate cost-per-square-foot for one of the 1,200 sq.ft. ranch-house plans in the following chapters, that 8-TimberTruss set would be about a $5,500 parts cost. This comes to $4.70/sq.ft. The 2×8 roof decking, see fig. 3.6A, nailed directly on top of the trusses, creates the interior exposed vaulted ceiling. Is this stronger and attractive structure worth the extra few dollars per square foot? The alternative is to use 7/16"-thick OSB for the roof underlayment and to use 1/2"-thick *Sheetrock* for the ceiling in the typical home. The difference in struc-

Fig. 3.6A Single Timber Truss bedroom with 5/12-20' truss

tural strength between these two construction approaches is significant, especially with an approaching hurricane or tornado. Let's look at the benefits of Timber Truss construction.

Here's where a <u>key crossroads level decision must be made</u>. The Timber Truss style will be presented and shown to be a simple, efficient, cost-effective method of home construction. If the reader wants a typical suburban, flat ceiling, sheet-rocked home; that <u>is not covered here</u>. The two principal structural modules, SIP walls and Timber Trusses, as presented here, is what differentiates these construction methods from traditional construction methods. The focus here is on structural quality and integrity, and simple, but versatile designs.

GABLE END CONSTRUCTION:

Gable end interior structural 2×6 walls must match the Timber Truss shape. They can be divided up into two halves: trapezoid shaped upper quadrants plus the centered 6×6 ridge post, that is the seat for the interconnecting horizontal top ridge 6×6 ridge beam that spans the trusses from gable-end wall to gable-end wall, and the lower, typically 8'-high framed wall

- Quadrants can be shop built using a tooling jig to maximize fast assembly and ensure consistency in shape
- Middle 6×6 pine post matches the Timber Truss ridge beam seat height

As shown in fig. 3.6B, the top gable wall section that sits on the top plate of wall is constructed in three sections or modules:

Left and right trapezoid-shaped sections and a center ridge pine post, which is a 6×6 that is 54" tall.

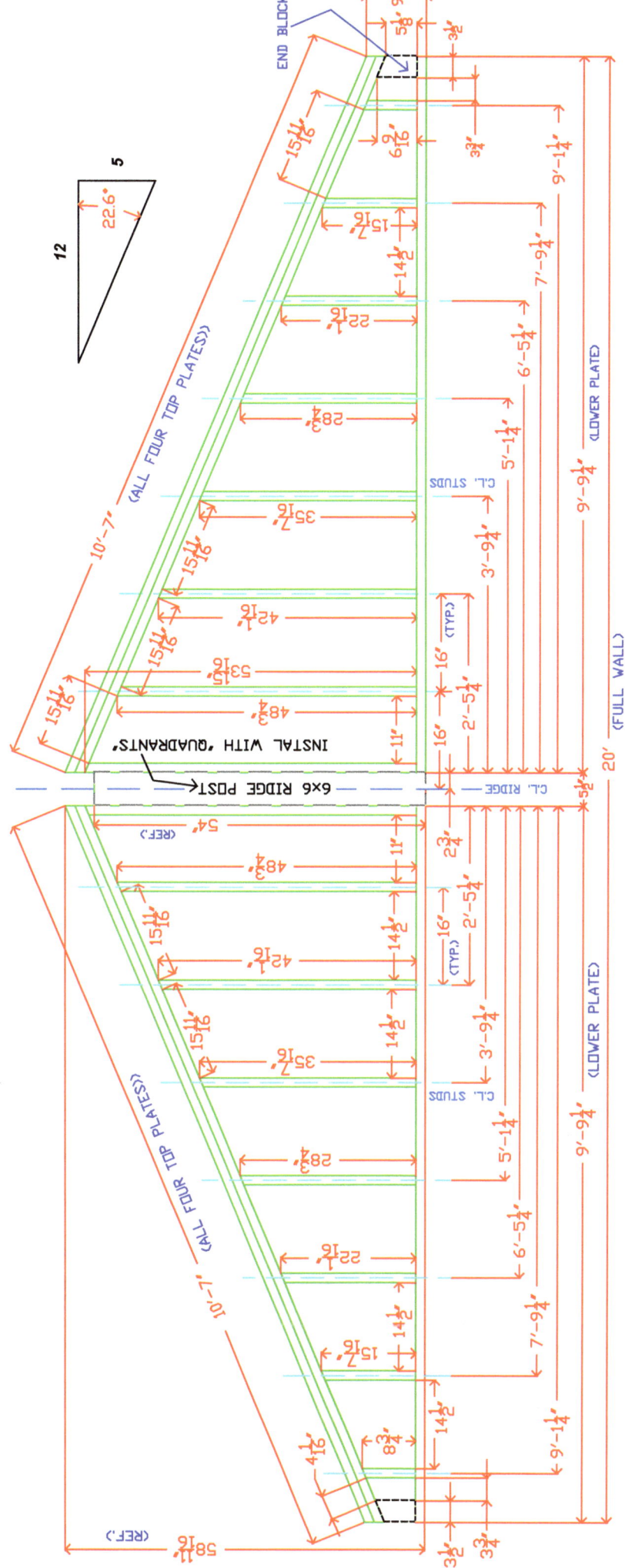

FIGURE 3.6B Full gable end wall top section drawing.

Fig. 3.7 The gable-end section assembled in the jig.

Fig. 3.8 The gable-end section removed from the jig. Note that a second top plate has been attached to this section, adding additional strength to the gable end.

Fig. 3.9 Completed gable end on house.

Since the left and right trapezoidal section are identical in shape and construction, the same tooling jig can be used to make both, at a cost of about $100 for materials to make the jig.

Fig. 3.9 shows the 6×6 vertical ridge post installed between the two trapezoidal sections. This post sets the height for the 16' long, 6×6 ridge beam that connect the truss tops and the gable walls at each end. After the Timber Trusses have been installed, the ridge beams are secured to these ridge posts and in the King truss centers using *TimberLOK* screws.

Now contrast this sub-assembly process to on-site built gable ends, which are hand-framed the standard way as shown in fig. 1.21. That version had to be hand-modified later because it was not accurate. Building sections using a jig, accuracy is achieved each and every time.

The labor needed to build the gable-end sections and assemble them on site, for a 9-gable house, using a four-man framing crew:

- Time to build the 18 sections in jig: averaging about 15 minutes or less for each section, comes to about 4 hours labor.
- Time to install on walls: about 3-4 hours total
- The total install time was less than 4 hours boom truck time because all the parts fit together perfectly. Traditional stud-wall and gable-end construction on site requires more time, and usually with less accurate results.

As noted earlier, the exterior gable-end walls need to match the profile of the Timber Truss beams. 6"-thick SIPs are generally used to create most or all exterior walls. The SIP versions of gable-ends will also need to match the Timber Truss profile. Usually the SIP gable-ends are built to include the entire shape. To make a 20' wall, typically three vertical SIP sections are used: Two at 8' wide and one at 4'-wide. These sections are assembled flat and then lifted into place with a boom truck.

The homes/floorplans in this book use vaulted

Fig. 3.10 Completed full gable end wall SIP section

ceilings with a Timber Frame interior. Selecting the roof decking to safely span the 64" gaps becomes the next decision. For this we choose #2-grade eastern white pine, in a 2×8 configuration (typically 16'-long pieces).

CEILING/ROOF UNDERLAYMENT:

To see the details described below, see fig. 3.17. 2×8 T&G decking is attached to the top of the Timber Trusses and gable walls with #16 framing nails. Typical framing attaches OSB roofing underlayment using #10 roofing nails[6].

- Code books generally allow using #2-pine wood, which results in a solid structure well above the code standard of 20#/sf traditionally framed homes
- Nailing from above allows for faster installation than from below, which entails cutting and fitting all the thinner, 3/4"-thick material used in typical construction, for cosmetic, not structurally-stronger roofs
- The thicker 2×8 decking enables the SIP panel screws to go through the top 1/2"-thick roof sheathing and down through the 2-layer, 9-1/4"-thick R38 foam panels and secured into the T&G decking underlayment
- Results in a very strong, beautiful roof, inside and out, that will likely not be destroyed in severe weather, including tornadoes
- Labor costs for installing this 2×8 T&G in our southeast U.S. region is about $1-$2/sq.ft., depending on the decking supplier's location

R38 ROOF INSULATION:

Two layers of 4×8 sheets and some 2×8 sheets to create staggered/offset joints of 4-5/8" thickness that meets R38 insulation code for many U. S. Energy Codes, southern to mid-state zones[7].
Installation is quick if using the proper cutting tool, which is a 4' hot-wire foam cutter on a table with 90° and 5/12 roof pitch guides. Overlap both horizontal and vertical joints between lower and top layers. Foam is installed over the *Titanium®* synthetic underlayment, using

Fig. 3.11 First rows of 4/12 roof 2×8 decking installation. The crew has installed the first few courses of decking in the morning.

staples, not typical cap nails.
- 1/2"-thick CDX plywood on top completes this triple-sandwich structure.
- 11" *HeadLOK* panel screws go through plywood, both foam layers and into the 1-1/2"-thick, 2×8 T&G roof decking taking care to avoid panel screws coming through at the V-joints in T&G. The installed screws will go into the T&G decking 1-1/4", ensuring a solid installation of all roofing materials.
- The CDX plywood top layer is covered with *W. R. Grace Ice & Water Shield*®.

ROOF DECKING PROCESS

The following photos show how the roof materials are installed. This wedge-shaped, 24' long, slightly less steep, 4/12 pitched Timber Trusses are easy to climb the roof and are similar to the smaller, 5/12-20' gable-style roof trusses for the homes shown later.
- The T&G five-man installation crew, contracted out as one job, started about 8am
- 2×8, #2 white pine decking, 16' lengths for 64" truss/wall spacing, (3-64" SIPs = 16')
- T&G decking is nailed to the Timber Trusses and gable walls #16 framing nails using an air gun nailer
- Crew added most of the structural blocking around the perimeter for aiding in installing EPS foam insulation
- Roof area is about 1,700sq.ft.
- Time needed to complete the roofing structure was 4-1/2 hours
- The sub-contract cost was $1800 or about $1.00/sq.ft.

Using SIPs for roofing is not recommended. Experience has shown that the modular approach of using larger roof SIPs may appear to be good, but the fitting the very large panels on roofs proves to be labor intensive, and boom truck time really adds up.
- Installing the 2×8s decking, the two EPS foam layers, and the 1/2" CDX top sheathing costs about $6-$7/sq.ft. A 10"-thick SIP costs $8-$10/sq.ft. just for materials, installation costs are in addition to material costs. The resulting roof strength for the

Fig. 3.12 After the first several rows of T&G, the interior appearance is really now displaying its beauty! Note the T&G spans over not only the Timber trusses, but the matching-profiled 2×6 framed interior gable structural walls.

Fig. 3.13 Exterior view of 2×8 decking near mid-point.

- sandwich installation is in the same ballpark the SIPs, perhaps even stronger
- The two boom truck sessions are needed for the SIP roof, with trusses installed first, then the time gap for the 2×8 installation, then the second boom truck session for installing the roof SIPs makes for awkward scheduling
- Then the bottom sides of the roof SIPs still need to be finished on the interior of the house, either fitting 3/4" pine between rafters or installing *Sheetrock*
- General contractors are learning about SIP construction techniques, which can give a balanced approach to blending different technologies in the right portions

ALTERNATIVE ROOF INSULATION

- Nail base roof panels are SIP-like but have only the top OSB panel bonded to the foam insulating panel
- Need 9-1/4" foam thickness as noted earlier
- Attach with panel screws also into the thicker 2×8 T&G
- Need a full set of roof plan shop drawings for the several panels types needed
- Rough cost estimates not much below full SIPs about $1-$2/sq.ft. less
- For the smaller 5/12 -20' roof run of about 11'-long, 4'-wide panels can be handled by crew of two
- This will work and has potential but the 2×8 T&G decking is the deciding factor

54   CHAPTER THREE

Fig. 3.14 Underlayment installation on 2×8 roof decking.

Fig. 3.15 With the decking complete and the protective underlayment in place, the crew is now installing the vertical perimeter boards (blocking). This blocking sets the proper height for the roof insulation panels (typical for our projects is 9-1/4" high, 2×10 depth, for R38 energy code.

RECOMMENDED RESIDENTIAL SUB-SYSTEMS:

Mini split ductless HVAC systems

- These have no HVAC ducting and the units can be used in major rooms using the outdoor compressor subsystem
- They can be single indoor dual, triple, etc., as best fits house plan layout specifics
- Bathrooms only need small wall/baseboard heater with a thermostat control and not a full indoor unit
- Some premier suppliers i.e., *Mitsubishi Electric*, provide systems with three different indoor unit load ratings using just one outdoor compressor i.e., 6,000, 9,000, or 12,000 BTUs that can match different room sizes/loads more optimally[8]
- Preferred supplier: *Mitsubishi Electric*

Fresh air EVVs (Energy Recovery Ventilator)

- Installed in one or two bedrooms per floor plan needs
- Brings fresh air in and cycles stale air out which these tight homes need
- Prefer spot version rather than complex ducted versions
- Preferred supplier: *Panasonic*

MODULARITY WHAT & WHY 55

Energystar *Bathroom Exhaust Fans*

One properly sized per bathroom
Preferred vendor: *Panasonic*

Water Heater Lifetime Tank

- Electric, not gas, with life-time plastic tank, not a metal tank with typical grade coating
- Preferred vendor: *RHEEM* Marathon-series tanks and not more complex heat-pump types

House Energy source: Total Electric, Not Gas

- Prefer no combustion in these tight homes
- Many cooks prefer to use gas for cooking, but in tight homes the impact of extra carbon monoxide and dioxide from the stove is an issue that should be considered
- Typical total electric monthly costs of these homes in mid USA will be about $100/month, less for smaller versions of these homes in the southeast thus, gas for just cooking?
- Electric water heating monthly cost is $15-$20 using gas would mean a small savings but not worth the combustion safety issues
- Use *EnergyStar* rated appliances
- Use LED lights wherever practical

Utility Chase is near Top Plate in Great Room

- With SIP walls and slab foundations on one-level floor plans, and ductless mini split HVAC, utility chase aids in connecting the whole house with electric, HVAC freon bundle, and water pipes
- Typically the chase is 12"×12" plus Timber Truss heel height (as needed) that runs horizontally with the bottom at 7' off the floor (see fig. 3.16)
- Integrates with kitchen cabinets attaching under the chase
- Some plans have adjacent coat or pantry closets, utility chase adapts to those profiles
- Great mounting space for indoor mini-split indoor unit, freon and, electrical runs adapt well here. Water lines can be run in chase, between two bedroom wings
- Recommend using wood panel access covers (not *Sheetrock*), at 36" – 60" centers for access

Windows and Doors

- Hi-grade exterior, prefer clad aluminum; fiberglass or vinyl windows will work
- Generally wood jamb interiors
- Strongly suggest paying for triple pane over current *EnergyStar* dual-pane minimums
- Minimize fancy shapes, mullions, etc.
- Prefer casement, awning, or fixed pane for centered-view window in triple windows, no single, double hung, or sliders)
- With Timber truss structural posts at 64" spacing, the triple window integrates well:
- Left flanking casement about 30" × 54"
- Middle fixed-view window is non venting and is 54"-60" wide by 54" high
- Right flanking casement 30" wide × 54" high
- Avoid tall 6'-high and skinny, double-hung window used by spec builders that can have issues with proper sun-shading control, particularly in passive solar homes
- Steel clad, foam insulated, *EnergyStar* rated exterior doors, not wooden doors
- Avoid double French patio doors or sliding glass doors like beach homes usually have

A very important set of features I generally employ in client's homes, when the chosen property allows it, is passive solar design. Passive is not an active, complex electrical system using PV solar panels. The house is designed to capture sun in colder months and block it out in warmer months. The season dictates where the sun energy goes. Several major techniques have to be followed properly to gain this natural energy. And the chosen building site must first have the ability to attempt this strategy.

Passive Solar Design Techniques

- Property site must have a south-facing,

- sloping terrain
- House shape is a rectangle with long wall for windows on south side. House runs along an east-west axis
- Floor plan should maximize window area on long south wall and minimize windows as much as practical on the other three sides
- Typical 150-170 sq.ft. of total window area in a small ranch house, goal is to get about 100-120 sq.ft. of that total on the south wall

Window Specifics:

- Best if triple pane, but minimum dual-pane *Energystar* rated window will work
- Best height around 54" tall and casement style, or fixed pane where practical
- Prefer more total width, not height
- South overhang window shading calculated per location but typical lengths are 20-28"
- Can relax the southern window code requirement for solar blocking because windows are properly shaded in summer

MAXI Ranch plan example

- 1,173 sq.ft. in 20' × about 59' footprint
- 166 sq.ft. window total, 139 sq.ft. on south wall, 27 sq.ft. north, no east or west windows
- South windows generate about 209,000 BTUs on typical sunny winter day[9]
- Translates to about 8,700 BTU/hour over 24-hour period (about ¾ ton)
- The house load calculations as per J-Manual is in the 1-1.3-ton unit range
- Passive solar gain in winter days equals a large portion of heating needs
- Must have substantial thermal mass
- With energy gain noted above, a significant mass is needed to absorb heat and store it so it can be used to control temperature swings
- If not enough thermal mass you just have uncontrolled heat gain and your HVAC system has to work more to bring that excess temperature gain back to a comfortable level
- Most practical approach is slab floor, insulated under and on edge where code allows
- Several southern states do not allow EPS foam under slab because of termite path issues. Some new products like *Foamglas®* made by *Owens Corning*, should now enable under-slab insulation. A minimum of 4-6 sq.ft. of floor slab is needed per window area. An entire slab floor is the best scheme[10].

How does Passive Solar work

The reader may understand passive solar if I use my own house, located in north Georgia near Appalachian Mountains. It's a retirement-oriented Wedge-design house. A quick summary of structure is:

- 1,536 sq.ft. on main floor in 24' × 64' rectangle with a wedge-shaped 4/12 truss on roof
- Insulated 4-5"- thick, concrete slab floor on R10, hi-density EPS insulation on a steel structure, elevated, insulated, and sealed crawl space
- R22 spray foam 2×6 walls
- R44 roof that is above *EnergyStar* local code and close to DOE (department of energy) Net-Zero Energy specs
- Non-vented roof structure is almost identical to described; about one more inch or EPS foam needed
- Triple-pane windows equaling 180 sq.ft. on south, about 12 sq.ft. on north, and none on east and west 22" window overhang
- Ductless mini splits *Mitsubishi* triple system, 1-12K BTU, 1-9K, and 1-6k indoor units
- HVAC calculation per J-Manual was about 1.1 tons of heat pump needed
- With more land elevation drop than preferred and boundary limit issues, I had to shift the house about 15° more southeast than the preferred 0-5° to southeast so some potential gain was lost, particularly after midday

Results on cool day with the above parameters:

- Overnight low dropped to 41° in mid-October 2019

Fig. 3.16 Indoor HVAC mini-split in middle of utility chase.

- The HVAC was turned off
- At evening the house inside temperature was about 73° before first cold night
- Morning inside temperature had dropped to about 71.5°
- By 11am it was up to 72.9° by 12:30pm temperature was 73.8°, and, 74° by 3pm
- By 8pm house was 73.8° with the next overnight outside low at 45°
- The next morning the house was 71.6°, a 2.2° drop with HVAC off for almost two days

We normally do not have the HVAC system off, but this situation was due to the rapid switch of an unusually long, hot fall and then a quick overnight shift to cool. I was testing to see how the house works. This shows how a passive solar house performs.

How does this play out in my monthly power bills? For about the first three years, our power bill averaged about $82 per month which is about 670KW/month. This is with total electric, including pumping our water from a well and electric water heating. I'm very confident my temperature variation is far more consistent and comfortable than the average house built per code. During this same period, the 1,900 sq.ft., 3-bed/2-bath house shown in many of the photos in this chapter, their first power bill was $114 using 838 KW/month, even with two youngsters.

INDUSTRY TRAINING

It is amazing to me that with all the recent year's press coverage about the upcoming millennial generation's huge student debt load (about $1.6 trillion now or about $37 thousand each[11]) and the counter-balancing blue-collar trade training side of this issue is not discussed much. In fact the only reasonable voice on the need for more blue-collar-trades training is Mike Rowe of the *Dirty Jobs* television show. His experience out in the field far overwhelms all the so-called experts and even academia's explanations. Mike has a foundation to give blue-collar training scholarships[12].

Why is contrast of these two issues so im-

portant in the residential construction industry?
- Too many generic degrees, and many non-graduates, and their resulting career pay is not close to costs of their education.
- Construction tradesman need more training. Fundamental flaw in career planning advice given by media and academia:
  1. Experts quoted that 50-70%, or more, of future jobs require college degrees.
  2. Basic soft skills need more attention in high schools, i.e., wood shop, auto body repair, electrical work, metal working, drafting/CAD, and computer software introduction.
  3. Many business staffs, generic offices, medical offices, retail, etc. will quickly disprove the over-glamorized degree needs.
  4. Numerous liberal college first-year-hire salaries average $30-$40k in 2019. This is in the range of many blue-collar trades.
  5. Electrical, plumbing, HVAC, and new-car techs exceed these salary levels.
  6. Shortage of labor in the trades while excess of generic degrees in journalism (75,000 in 2010, about 23 for each of the approximately 3200 counties in the USA per year), sociology, psychology, and some art specific majors[13].

In our immediate, small, 3-person family we have five degrees:
- I have BS in Engineering
- My wife has a BS in Nursing and two masters degrees, including Nursing practitioner.
- My daughter has a Doctorate in Pharmacy

We were exposed, thanks to our parents, to many activities while young and were able to work toward specific careers choices that we were fairly confident of. We didn't get any general liberal arts degree and expect the world to come to our doorstep with rewards. I have had many young relatives and friend's children recently going through this life's dilemma without the level of direction that we had.

Consumer Reports did an article in August 2018 with the cover noting: *I kind of ruined my life by going to college*. With 42 million Americans with student debt, this is not a trivial situation[14].

Without better training in the blue-collar trades, improvement in the quality of work, and not learning much about new approaches to improve the industry, i.e., SIP modular construction, won't happen at a needed pace. The average framer has been taught on-the-job and he only knows that amount. Many senior framers I have noted are still weak in reading drawings. And yet, they are usually frozen in what they have learned from that one source and are resistant to change or improve. I recently had a framing crew leader tell me that he, "Did not care" that there was a better, faster, way to build some of the house assemblies, like the gable section's jig just noted.

Here's another example of a simple process improvement using the gable section jig. Some of the framer sub's use 12-16'-long covered trailers with reasonably organized bins, etc. Many use my preferred 12" sliding compound miter saw and not just 7-1/4" power hand saws. I have much experience as a sawman too, not just doing CAD on the computer. I'm amazed how some have the portable compound saw tables they set up in the yard, but don't go the next step. My next step is to design and build a light, metal, fold-down saw table mounted on the left side of the trailer. It would flop down and swing out on adjustable legs. It would have a rear feed and exit back stop with a system to quickly set different lengths when running multiple cuts, far more accurate than hand saws. The building of the gable-end section in the jig would make this production set up of those 5/12 top short studs fast. The John Henry myth that hand-made is better sometimes isn't true.

This saw set-up example points to one common observation noted over decades in multiple projects, in multiple states, and with many different teams: the tradesman rarely have any exposure to other industries that could be beneficial. A specific detail is that many tradesman do not realize if you don't follow the designer's drawing in many non-construction industries you may get fired. Commercial construction with required Professional Engineer (PE) stamps tend to bring this to focus there. With better blue-collar training at a trade school program, the skill level of the worker is exponentially better and they can understand fundamental business practices. This training can lead to better pay for them. Why is better training and continual process improvement important? Check out the history of the U. S. automotive industry after World War II and on through the growth, changes, and challenges of the next few decades. The massive success of Japan's car industry at the same period as the U. S. declines mirrors this issue. And now South Korea's pattern is similar. Contrast those two countries improving car industries and the lack of improvement in the U. S. residential construction; the handling of materials slows the construction process.

Due to the high-value feature of the beautiful Timber Trusses over conventionally engineered trusses 2×4s from high-volume truss shops, I have strongly advised my clients to be well prepared to cover the trusses during all the phases of construction. I have specifically noted they need to have a full set of tarps ready to go to cover the trusses after initial install and before the protective roof materials are installed. In fact, I tell them to cover them up immediately after installation regardless of weather predictions. It is amazing how much resistance one gets from the typical contractor or framing crew on this. Evidence again of poor preparation. An even better example of a recent project involved regular 2×4 trusses delivered to the site: They were left on bare, wet ground, and not covered up through a couple of rains before I advised the client to cover them several days later. The result: black mold on the lower truss chord of several of the trusses. They were then installed and not even cleaned up. Black mold is a bad thing for your health; check with some liability lawyers. I have many examples of crews, general contractors, or the owners not covering up or stacking the materials properly at the end of the work day. Do you think the final quality for the completed house will somehow spring positively from these processes?

Since I was a CO-OP student in engineering school and worked seven quarters in an aircraft design/assembly environment in a wide variety of departments, before graduating, I had a huge range of exposure to many processes, job assignments, etc. Then, the early part of my design career involved small companies where a variety of skills from electronics to plastics to metals was terrific exposure.

This discussion is not about anti academia and not politically bent. It is a sincere observation that I am convinced history will finally expose over time. We are out of balance in the U. S. on where our training and education efforts and dollars are going. Not only the student loan debt monster, the shortage of skilled workers for non degreed trades, and then factoring in the significant number of online and landed college closures should be more than adequate to signal something ominous is occurring.

Frankly, construction clients should be very cautious of design advice by subcontractors and contractors for these same reasons. Builders and framers generally only know some of the building codes, and not extensively. And the codes themselves are just minimum levels, like just barely passing with a D+. Most of these contractors or subs do not have any building science training and don't understand thermal/moisture house issues, i.e., vented roofs. One of the best recent examples is a contractor telling the client they don't need triple-pane windows for a passive solar house. They also suggested the client add a porch, which means longer roof across the south window. The client understood that over shading there would kill the winter sun gain and darken the house interior[15]. Despite the vast majority of well-intentioned, hard-working, good contractors out there, they can mislead a client without even knowing the future impact.

Another bad advice design change on a recent project was done by a trade generally with good training that should have caught this: the HVAC installation location of mini-split indoor unit. I had recommended both a specific vendor, the type of dual indoor system, two duals, and significantly the location of the indoor unit in the great room. These technical specifics were communicated to the general contractor, but

apparently not to the HVAC sub-contractor:
- Great room is long and thin at 20' × 36'.
- Utility chase, as noted earlier, runs along the north 36' room.
- I had recommended the indoor unit close to center of this long room, roughly between the dining and living zones (see fig. 3.16).
- Recommended two dual systems which means four indoor units for the entire house so the great room /master bedroom outdoor unit would balance short freon/electrical bundle lengths within the utility chase.
- My preferred supplier offers multiple systems of different indoor units load ratings, i.e., 12,000 BTU for the great room and 6,000-9,000 BTU for the master bedroom, or smaller bedrooms. (9,000 BTU, or ¾ ton, is the most popular indoor unit.)

The 2nd and 3rd bedroom's system was a smaller outdoor compressor with only the 6,000 BTU indoor units and a more compact, closer, utility bundle that runs to outside unit.

What was actually installed? The largest room indoor unit for the great room was installed at the very end of the 36' great room and its utility cable run came from the now, triple, outdoor compressor through the two smaller bedrooms. That cable run was fairly long. More complexity was added because the indoor unit was mounted where a planned wood stove pipe was intended. Even if the stove eventually is not used, it's potential option is checkmated by the HVAC indoor location. But there is an even more buried detail wrestled over by the designer (me) several months before the contractors even saw the floor plans. I suspect this detail was discovered very late in the building process that then led them down the poor path of the Indoor HVAC unit location. Some background on this design choice issue:

- The larger 1,900 sq.ft., ten truss, longer 6' spacings, layout was more difficult for Timber Truss locations than the 64" spaced Squashed-H plan, now 1,700 sq.ft., shown in Chapter 7.
- The large Timber Truss base had to be close to the end of the great room wall and the intersection to the second bedroom wing.
- This truss location effectively blocked a good path for the HVAC outdoor bundle from connecting to the already-built, utility chase along the long great room wall.
- Since the HVAC and/or the general contractor chose the triple indoor version (again, mine was two duals), this third indoor unit had to be located in the end wall of the great room and thus did not take advantage of the existing utility chase.
- Many details are involved in designing and not easily seen in the field during construction. Constant communication is needed.

I suspect that with the silliness of the dream house mentality of the housing industry and even flamed more by the saturation of Reality TV shows, there may be a cynical overreaction by the trades guys. That is, they have seen many cutesy house designs by architects and residential designers that are difficult to build and not well thought out. Even DOE Housing Energy chief, Sam Rashkin's book noted in chapter 1 addressed this over-decorated, current homebuilding approach. Sam is an experienced architect and ran the EPA's *EnergyStar* program successfully for years. But design issues can be very complex.

Design honesty and integrity

One last topic involving the design phase of residential construction also bears some discourse, particularly when contrasted to the upcoming six floor plan examples. That is integrity. For example, I am a strong supporter of Green Building. But my bent is of the practical Green focus. Having designed and built (actually physically built and not just contracted) *Energystar* certified and equivalent homes; designed, built, and lived in three passive solar homes for 38 + years; written a book on one *EnergyStar* project, *Building Today's Green Home*, and being certified as a LEED-AP for more than twelve years, I believe this is a valid background to comment here. In contrast, I have seen many shows, online and in print articles, of projects that profess to be Green when the house size is in the 3,000 sq.ft. size and larger. They also have many of the silly, curb-appeal-only cosmetic decorations just discussed. For example, one particular project featured in a cover article had almost 4,000 sq.ft. with five bedrooms and six bathrooms, and a large basement area for many wine bottles. And despite all its certifications, in the end, this is not really Green. Green is practical. The design must demonstrate honesty and integrity or its impact will be wasted effort. We offer simple floor plans as our attempt to do just that.

THE BOTTOM LINE:

Before showing several floor plans using the above described building concepts, I offer one more drawing showing the typical roof construction of most American suburban homes and the key sub-module Timber Truss for the roof subsystem. I suggest the reader ponder the news media reporting pattern and the housing industry reactions of the tornado/hurricane bad news that results:

- Emotional still photos and videos of the huge path of destruction.
- Talk of, "We need to make homes more resilient."
- But what actually happens? Code and government changes and industry shifts take years or decades.
- Many architects and journalists write stories, comment, and show some examples, but we seem to only have the "alleged" advanced framing example just elaborated on with no real change.
- Millions and millions of American homes have the typical structure as shown on the left side of fig. 3.17.
- We keep adding to this stockpile with fancier details to decorate the homes, i.e., tray ceilings, crown molding, etc.

The last decade or two of improvements using engineered roof trusses made in a factory are only cost improvements with smaller 2×4 components and press-in thin metal plates despite their PE certifications. Again, only cost and labor improvements, and no significant roof strength increase. In fact, the truss spacing widens to 24" on center vs. hand-framed 16" on center, and using the same thin 7/16"-thick roof sheathing.

I have seen dozens and dozens of suburban home subdivisions under construction in many of the north Atlanta boom communities for decades, all stretching the specific 2×6, long rafter example shown in fig. 3.17. In fact, many have stretched these long rafters to almost non-standard lengths of 18'- 22' to achieve the extremely steep 10/12 and 12/12 roof peaks. I could even see the camber droop in many of those rafters. Yet the codes have only started limiting those spans in the last few years.

Fig. 3.17 shows the conventional hand-framed roof structure that is similar to the 2×4 newer engineered, factory-built trusses, and my Timber Truss approach for a smaller, stronger, and better homes. Again, I leave the readers to ponder over which roof structure technology would you prefer during the last ten seconds before the tornado approaches or a hurricane is wailing outside? Would you be okay with just 7/16" of OSB sheathing and ½" *Sheetrock* between you and your family to the outside world as shown on the left side of the drawing? Or would you be more comfortable with almost 2" of pine decking, 9" of foam, and another 1/2" of CDX plywood, all sandwiched together on big beams with large, long, high-strength screws, as shown on the right side of the drawing?

This roof structure's cost is $5-$7 more per sq.ft., just a small increase for the entire house costs. For a few dollars more, think about it.

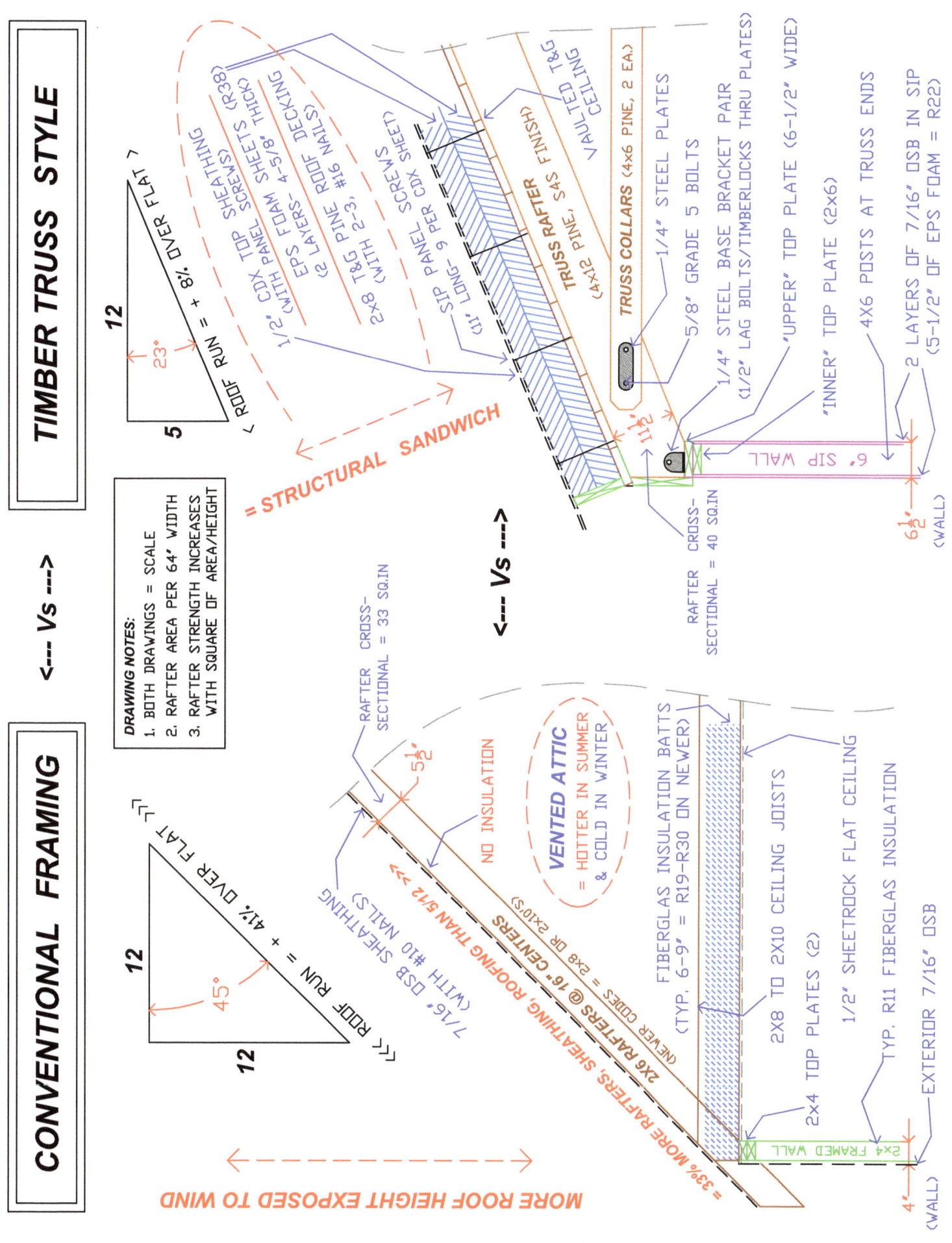

FIGURE 3.17 Conventional roof framing vs. Timber Truss style

chapter four

Vaulted ranches

We should begin with what is likely a Deja Vue experience for most of the Baby-Boomer readers here: What? Ranches? Again? Didn't we see this story in the 1950s through the 1970s as American suburbia exploded ? Yup, and the same reason then applies now: Ranches are practical. They are easy to build (faster and less labor, costs), cost less in materials, and are generally space efficient for their size if some modern floor plan layout concepts are applied. Remember our primary goal is practical downsizing.

But we have a major new feature here not often seen in the Suburbia Boom days: Vaulted, Timber Trussed, majestic, interior ceilings. This design twist adds a major jump in both the appearance of volume and attractiveness as pictured in the modules detailed explanations. Then add the enhanced structural integrity. So we just don't have your typical baby-boomer ranch happening again here. Remember that our focus is shifting from the exterior curb-appeal exaggeration back to enhancing the interior, where we actually spend most of our time.

We will present two examples of the vaulted ranches: The MINI, a 960 sq.ft., 2 bedroom, 2 bathroom with a 20' × 48' footprint with 6 Timber Trusses. The MAXI, a 1,173 sq.ft., 2 bedroom, 2 bathroom layout 20' × 58' - 8" footprint with 8 Timber Trusses.

We will begin with the smaller MINI, the epitome of the extreme practicality intended with this floor plan. That is, we have really a nice mini home, not a silly, faddish, too small tiny home. But, because of the practical thrust here, we have to optimize space everywhere. We don't need to go to the extremes of tiny homes where the typical loft bedroom and resulting access stairs are just beyond awkward and even dangerous for our mature clients. We have to be practical in trade offs in the smaller of two plans.

The reader should also note an important set of details included in these floor plans. We show typical realistic furniture sizes, with clearance dimensions noted in key walk-path zones. I have experienced many homeowners assuming the typical plans of rooms on paper and then finding out later upon moving in, that even standard size furniture will not fit. On the other hand, a realistic mindset by the new owner should balance the downsizing goal. For example, in the smaller home's second bedroom, is a queen or king size bed make sense now? Again, "makes sense" and not "luxury" features that would be normal in a larger, mid-life, family-sized home. The second bedroom is usually intended for the occasional guest, not full-time occupancy.

EXAMPLES OF REALISM IN THE MINI RANCH:

1. Master bedroom is reasonable 12'×16' (rough) layout
2. Master bath reasonable, but not intended as luxurious space (not have both shower and tub)
3. Master closet has one side larger for one of couple's major space user
4. Second bedroom is slightly smaller than the typical 10'×12' cabin-type rooms seen in north Georgia, southeast region, etc.
5. Could fit small computer desk zone in second bedroom
6. Second bath layout is a compact apartment-type layout using the 60" end-room-tub/shower scheme
7. Dining area permits about a 4-person size table, 36"× 60" or round 42"d.
8. Kitchen zone could have small extra bar counter but would be tight, possibly small, cart-like.
9. General strategy is for a retired couple with occasional guest or two 2nd bedroom, queen bed is possible, but, practical full size is shown.

IN/OUT RATIO

There is some good here regarding open floor plans, and that is they are usually simpler to build (less walls, wiring, halls, doors, trim, finish, etc). I use simple math to compare the outside wall total length to the total interior walls as a rough gauge of how open a plan is. For an example, let's begin with the MINI ranch. Exterior wall length equals 136 linear feet (l.ft). Interior wall length equals 79 l.ft. The in/out equals 58%. This percentage indicates a particular floor plan is more open than one with the interior wall totals approaching 100% of the exterior walls. This quick estimate can show that a particular floor plan is more "open". The six upcoming floor plans have an open floor plan.

MINI RANCH HIGHLIGHTS (SEE FIG. 4.1):

- 960 sq.ft. (20' × 48' footprint), total of 6 Timber Trusses
- 2 bedroom, 2 bathroom layout
- Great room equals 427 sq.ft. (20' × 21'-4"), 3 Timber Trusses
- Master bedroom equals 205 sq.ft. (16' × 12'-8"), 2 Timber Trusses
- Guest bedroom equals 127 sq.ft. (10'-8" × 11'-10" plus entry), 1 Timber Truss
- Master bath equals 64 sq.ft.
- Master closet equals 52 sq.ft.
- Guest bath equals 62 sq.ft.
- Guest bedroom closet equals 11 sq.ft.

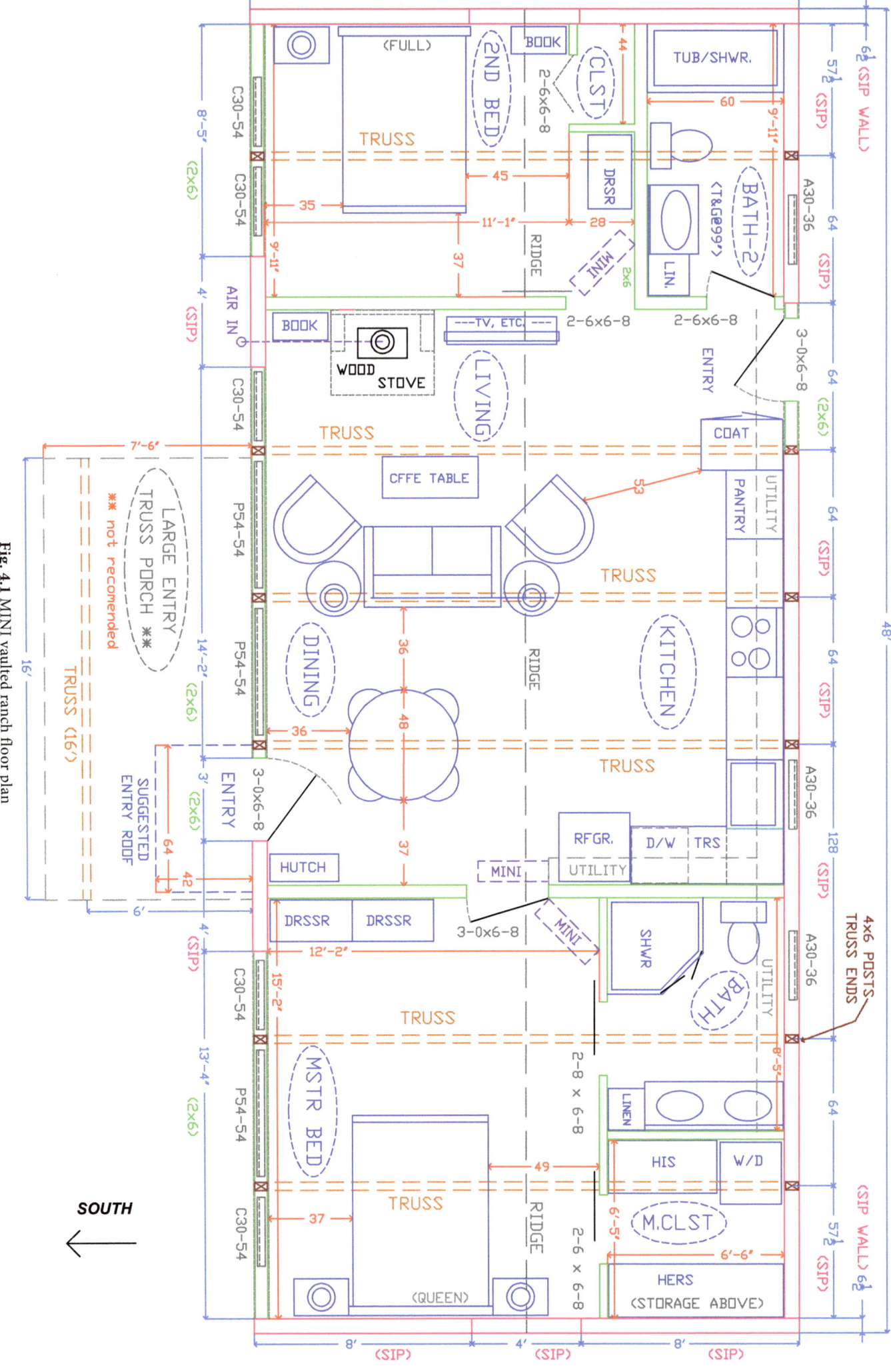

Fig. 4.1 MINI vaulted ranch floor plan

FRONT PORCH ADDITION

A quick glance at the MINI plan will note an extra feature not discussed earlier, nor will be added to the remaining floor plans: Timber Truss entry porch. We show it here as an important upgrade for this smallest plan. It adds a nice entrance to the interior trade offs already in the MINI plan. 20' Timber Trusses can be cut down to a 16'-wide version. The 2×8 T&G interior roof decking could be used on the porch roof as well as the house roof, with the best pieces used on the interior and the less attractive for porch. Wood protection for outdoor use should be used on the roof overhang.

Note that this added feature comes with two negative trade offs:
1. Loss of significant passive solar winter heat gain on a large part of the southern windows, as described in chapter 3. A majority of the following plans could utilize passive solar winter sun heat gain.
2. Darkening of the great room during daylight hours.

It is significant how this front porch cosmetic feature does enhance the home's street view. It elevates the basic ranch shape. This is also a perfect example of how cosmetic and practical features collide. In general, I tend to advise clients to go with the more practical solutions at this stage in one's life choices. A rear porch, if on the north side, has less impact. The owner needs to balance out these features for their overall housing goals. With this popular curbside gable protrusion view well known, we will skip an elevation view.

TECHNICAL WALL CONSTRUCTION

As was covered in detail in the previous chapter, the modularity building approach is utilized even in this smallest plan; that is, the two major module types, Timber Trusses and SIP wall modules are the bulk of the houses structure. Even the three-panel, 20'-wide, SIP gable is employed in the most basic manner, see fig. 3.10. Windows holes are not needed on this base model home. Note the east and west exterior gables as drawn here. SIP walls are shown using magenta-colored lines. The green-colored line walls along the south 48' wall are framed 2×6 walls.

The south framed 2×6 walls for the great room, about 15' long, the master bedroom, about 14' long, and the guest bedroom, about 6' long, are intended to be spray foam insulated (R22) later with the extra 7/16" OSB sheathing added to the inside before finishing to bring the total wall thickness to 6-1/2"-deep to match the SIPs.

The window and door headers need to be properly insulated also: either spray foam (drill 2 holes for foam nozzle in and out) or pre-made headers with pre-cut, 2-1/2"-thick, EPS foam panels in the header gap between the inner and outer header boards. R10 for EPS, up to R15 for higher-density foam panels with two-header thicknesses for a total R value of R13 or R18. The two small SIP sections at the great room gable ends at the transition to both bedrooms fits between the framed sections.

The benefits for 2×6 conventional framing vs. SIPs in this south wall, particularly with emphasis on labor efficient building strategy are:
- Framed modules are a manageable size to build, move, and can be stood up by a small crew
- Can be premade in advance in shop and transported; header sizes are modules also
- Framing around the entry doors enable easier wiring within the section; multiple electrical switches nearby, windows, corners, etc. The transition to SIPs at the house corners is facilitated to feed into SIP panel horizontal chases.
- The last framed-in entry-door section can account for any length variations of the balance of the full wall length. Allow and adjust for some variation in layout of door's rough opening jack studs locations
- The double-sided OSB, like the SIP style, are much stronger, tighter, and quieter than standard framing. Even without factoring, the spray foam over builder-grade-like fiberglass, etc. insulating materials

The larger great room framed section is detailed in fig. 4.2. I am using the rough openings recommended by *Jeld-Wen* clad aluminum windows, typically 3/4" over window frame size

"Alleged" advanced wall framing

And no, I don't recommend advanced framing, meaning 24" stud spacing, minimal headers, etc., which are not as strong and is cheaper. The math of the alleged insulation gains is trivial. Let's do a quick rough math comparison for the upcoming, larger, Maxi ranch house:

- Total south wall area equals 467 sq.ft. R22 for full SIPs
- Window area equals 140 sq.ft. with about a R2 rating
- Headers equal 31 sq.ft., R13 insulation
- Vertical studs and horizontal plate area equals 53 sq.ft. as built with SIP and frame hybrid
- *EnergyStar* door equals 21 sq.ft. R7

The weighted average of this wall is about R14. Of course, if the entire wall with SIPs with no windows or doors would be the maximum value of R22. This average drop from R22 to R14 is a result of several factors, not just the extra studs. The passive gain from these south windows contribute nearly a ton of heating value on winter days, far surpassing the energy losses from the lower R-values of windows. But the largest culprit by far is the *EnergyStar* level windows, double pane. I recommend triple pane. With respect to dropping the R value average of the wall, a typical cosmetic enhancement, usually added by such trendy enhancements, is a double French door, or even worse, a single-pane glass, wood-framed for appearance's sake only. This is even worse than the so-called gains of the weaker framing schemes.

One strategy employed, usually in grandiose example on designer homes on Reality TV, or magazine articles, is the floor-to-ceiling windows. Or even worse, the huge, folding, expensive, glass walls with the gotcha offering of bringing the outdoors inside. Which in non-tropical settings it means one thing: **COLD!** And the math here? Those huge glass walls/doors average about R2 rating vs. the R14-R22 walls noted above. Little that is given by these cosmetic charmers is practical things like losing short wall space for furniture, electrical receptacles, passive sun overhang shading, etc.

I have to wonder what schools teach this kind of math. Or even where fashionable building-advice articles online or print get their facts.

The south wall framing example I recommend is next. See fig. 4.2, facing page, as used in the larger MAXI plan.

Note the three large 54" × 54" picture windows (fixed, not ventilating) combined with the two outer casement 30"× 54" ventilating windows. This fairly extensive, but practical size (not floor to ceiling excess) sets up for good viewing, daylighting a Passive Solar Gain if the owner chooses to enable. And after my daughter's recent home search (many hours on *Zillow* alone!) in the Atlanta suburbs, there were very few homes that have this impressive window arrangement. In fact, a significant majority of the homes more than 20-30 years old have poor window examples even close to this "Little Ranch". And many in that typical American home market do not have windows that are large enough for the newer egress exit safety codes.

The highlight of the master bedroom is this three-window combination (see fig. 4.3 facing page) with the central picture and the two flanking casement (ventilating) windows. As just noted in the great room wall window pattern, this main bedroom set is far better than the typical suburban market just noted.

The guest bedroom framed window module is shown next (see fig. 4.4 following page). Note that the smaller room, by necessity, has to have a smaller window combination. But even here the two 30" × 54" casement windows are relatively nice for this smaller room.

The two additional small SIP modules (see fig. 4.4 on following page) shown on drawings as standard 4' SIPs, fit around the 2×6's ends of each wall section, with 1-1/2"- deep foam recesses to bury the end stud in each SIP module's recessed foam section to complete the full south wall.

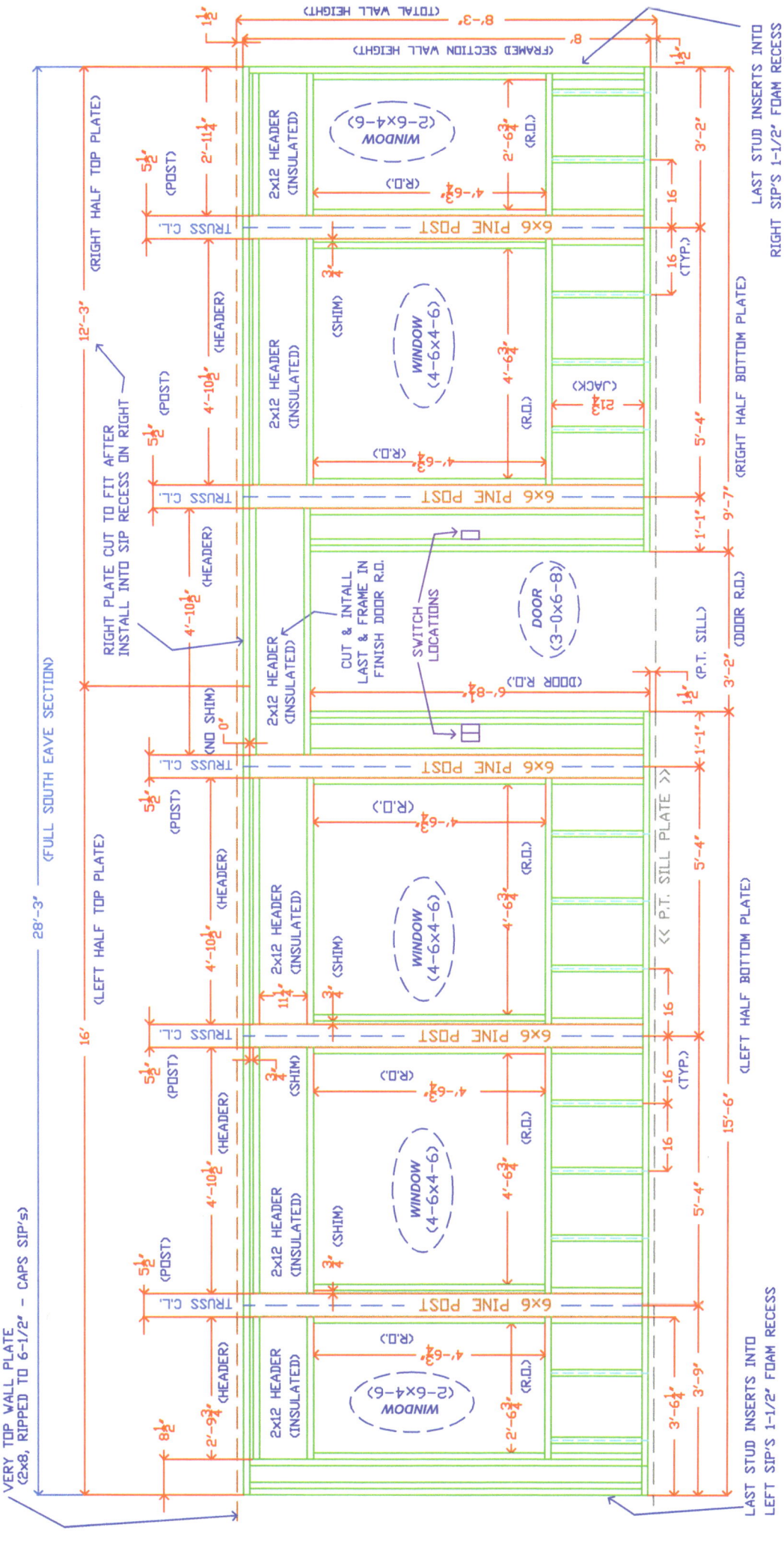

Fig. 4.2 South great room framed window

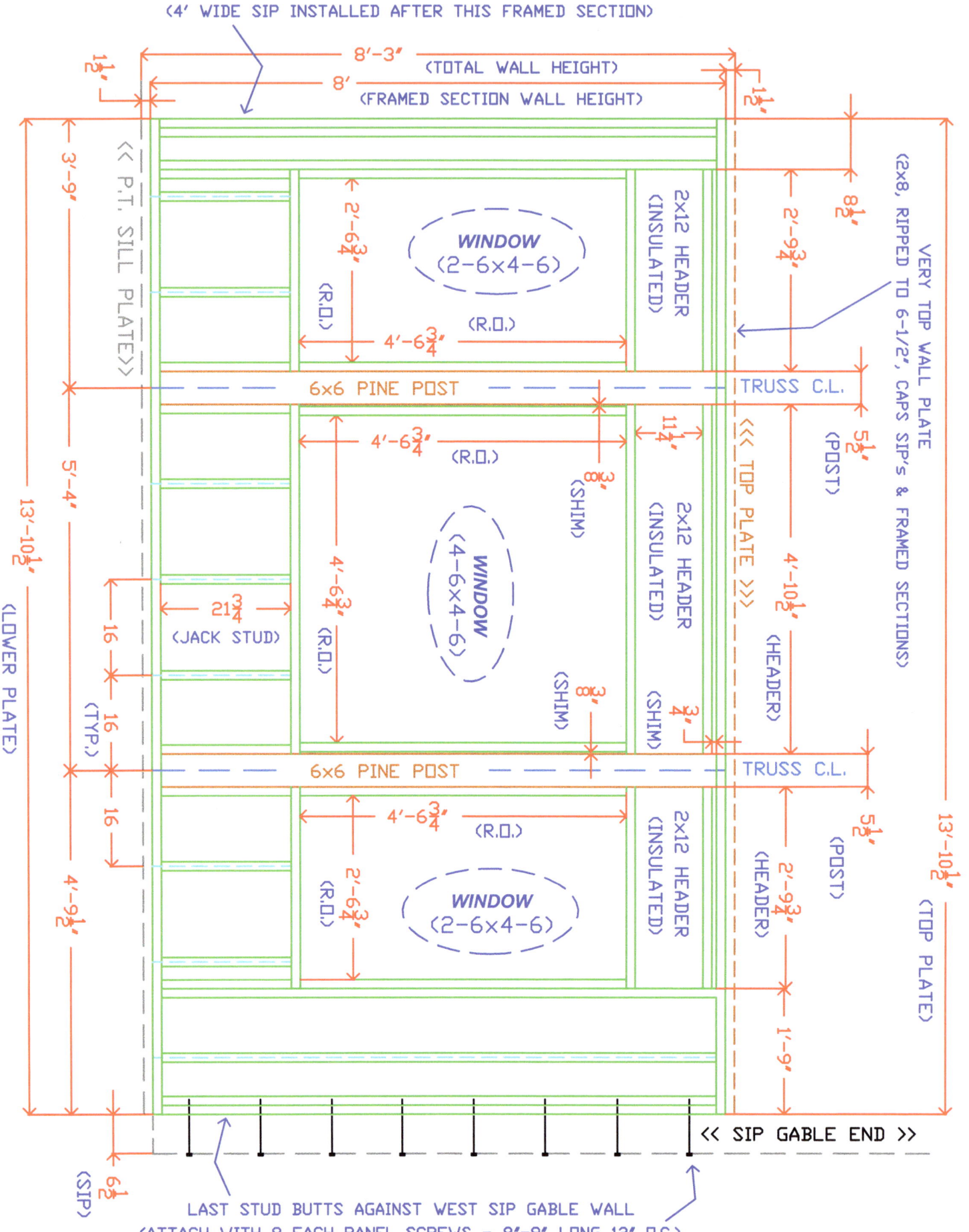

Fig. 4.3 South master bedroom framed wall section

MISC. CONSTRUCTION DETAILS:

3. Utility Chase:
- Built with 7' bottom, about 12" deep and can extend to the vaulted ceiling height, is generally shown on the north side and meshes with the kitchen cabinet's top heights
- Simple wood panels can cover access areas, 1×10 pine boards, 48-60" long
- Enables power, HVAC, and even some water lines
- Short shelves, about 4-6" out over the top kitchen cabinets can provide more display area
- Horizontal zones at foyer and master bath provide lighting locations
- Future emergency lighting, likely LED, with a 12VDC, not house 120 AC, battery backup can also be located in these horizontal zones
- Master bath, *EnergyStar* vent fan can also be located in this overhead horizontal plane and lead to easy vent exhaust to the exterior
- Most of the recommended ductless/mini-split HVAC freon/power lines can fit in the chase
- The great room mini-split indoor unit can also be mounted on the face of the utility chase
- Smaller (about 6"× 6") mini chases can connect to the main chase in the master closet (on back of storage shelf) and the second bedroom closet, and can be connected the mini-split lines to the main chase as needed

4. Storage ideas:
- Multiple, wide, storage shelves can be added, particularly in the master closet, about 6-8" above the hanging clothes
- The master version can use 2×4, 4×4 module at the 6-8" level and provide as wide as 24"-deep shelves
- Master closet shelves also can capitalize on the vaulted ceiling, possible second level nearer closet door?
- Both bathroom linen cabinets should capitalize on the standard 84"-tall, about 18"-wide, and 18"-deep vertical, stand-alone pre-made cabinets typically available

5. HVAC system suggestions:
- Strongly suggest ductless mini-splits for this size and energy efficient home
- *Mitusbishi* makes a triple unit with three different indoor unit ratings (6K btu, 9K btu, and 12K btu)
- Larger indoor unit in great room, medium in master bedroom, and smaller in second bedroom
- The triple-indoor system should work well in the smaller MINI ranch in order to keep the freon/power/condensation line bundle short enough for the single outdoor compressor located on the north wall near the kitchen window area. The indoor units need to be closer to the center of the house such as optimizing the bedroom indoor mounting with the 45° shelfs as implied in the plan. Also note the second shorter utility chase forming an "L" near the master bath wall to the master bedroom door.
- But in the larger MAXI ranch (128" longer great room) a single unit for the second bedroom and a dual for the master and great rooms may minimize the longest freon runs
- Compressor on north between kitchen and master bath, while the second, single version, compressor on east side just outside the 2nd bedroom closet. Note that the great room indoor unit needs to not be too close to the kitchen oven exhaust vent. Thus locating it along the longer north wall, closer to the entry door, but splitting the difference from door to vent.
- The two bathrooms don't really need air conditioning as the humidity exhaust function (*EnergyStar* rated fans) there is a priority, and would swamp the air in. Winter heat is best supplied with a small baseboard resistance heater (500-1,000 watts only) with a wall thermostat/timer control. Thus, these

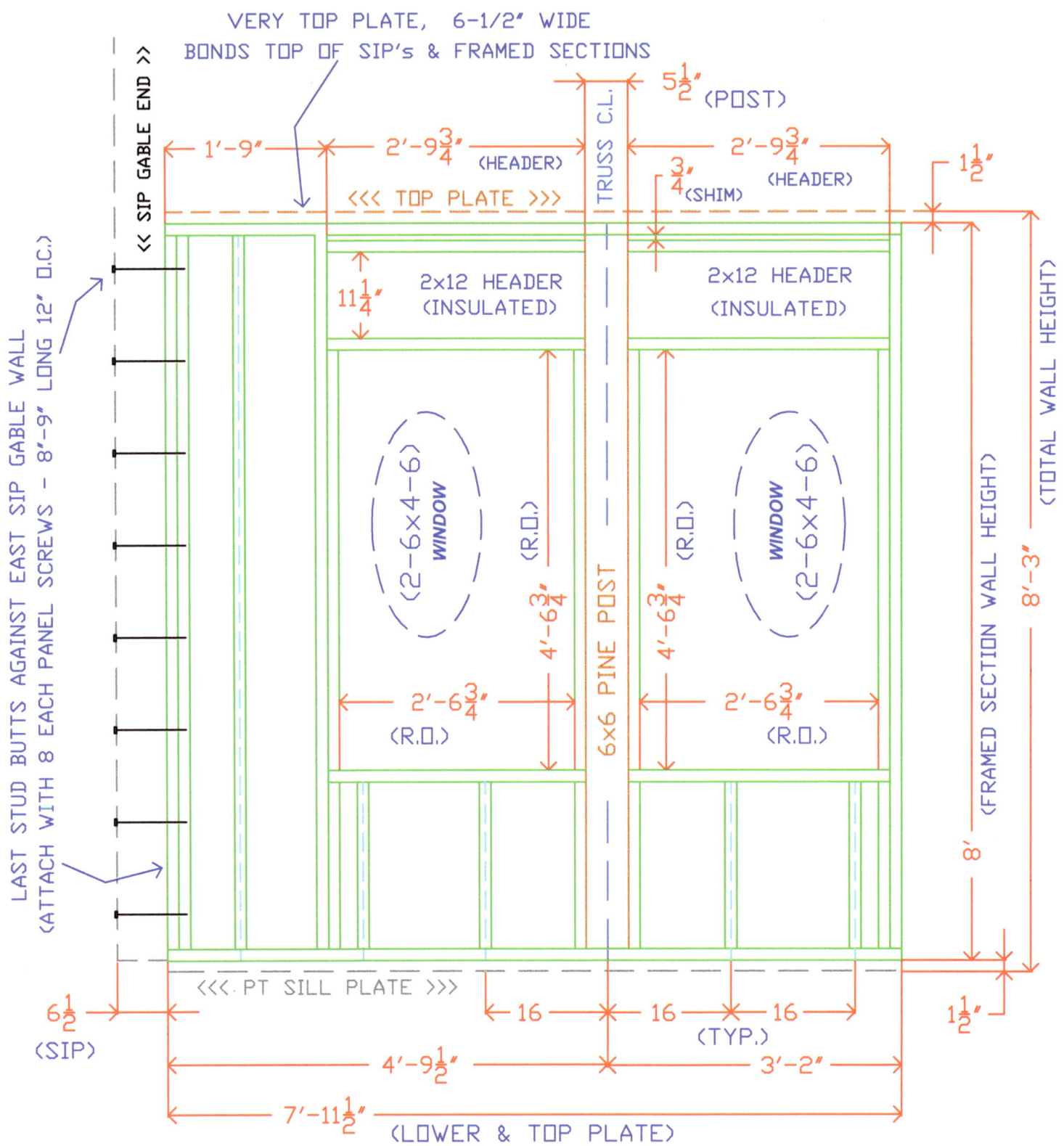

Fig. 4.4 South guest bedroom framed wall section

small heater units only need turning on in the winter months. The early morning turn-on/warm-up, feature in those colder months will be well received by the first morning riser.

6. Wood stove suggestions:

- The principal goal of the stove is emergency back-up heat, thus wood stove, not a gas fired unit is strongly recommended.
- New England has a nice small, glass windowed unit, EPA certified (Model 17-VL, retail about $750) with overall dimensions about 21" wide, 30" tall and 13" deep with a built-in log bin under the main fire section. A larger unit is not needed in these energy efficient homes; just 12"-long logs
- Note the external air vent under the stove and slab to the exterior, for combustion, not to use room air. Pipe with 3" diameter galvanized steel. Alternately, the air pipe can be on the back wall, just above the slab sill plate, installed later (wood trim to cover). The 3"-plus pipe hole can be drilled through the SIP wall during the brick surround construction. The air intake point on the stove is in the middle bottom of the firebox in the wood storage cavity under the firebox.
- This compact size enables a simple common brick surround on the back wall and one brick wide (8") plus the 6-8" gap around the stove back and sides to the brick. The surround only needs to be a couple of inches higher than the stove, a massive size is not needed here. The thermal mass from the brick around the stove will also temp the stove heat for hours.

7. Disability/wheelchair access issues:

- In these smaller homes, particularly the MINI ranch, meeting the full requirements of the ADA Disability standards is quite impractical. However, in places where we can enhance those needs, but not fully comply, such as the 2'-8" master bath door and the 3'-0" bedroom doors we do attempt a reasonable compromise. Note: many 1960's -1970's baby boomer ranches typically had 2'-4" and at most 2'-6" bedroom doors. Closets and baths even had 2'-0" doors.
- As the house sizes increase as the later floor plans unfold, the reader should note the ADA compliant options also improve.

Before moving on to the larger ranch version, a brief historical, yet personal, comparison on the smaller 960 sq.ft. MINI plan seems timely. My parents early 1960's ranch (now know as a baby boomer ranch) was a whopping 32' long by 24' wide. Which means folks, a total of 864 sq.ft., which is in the range of the typical house built then. And pile in several growing up boys for the full history accuracy. So now, we are suggesting that a retired couple only (two, just count em) could maybe manage on about another 100 sq.ft. feet? And, our small-town Alabama ranch did not look anything like the great room interior shown next as the larger 5-truss version in fig. 4.5. And I would feel much more secure in the fig. 4.5 timber truss house than the typical 2×4 framing of the earlier era, particularly with an Alabama tornado looming in the forecast!

THE MAXI VERSION RANCH:

The larger, MAXI version of this first vaulted ranch (see fig. 4.6 page 76) is simply the result of adding two more timber trusses to the great room (house center) section. This extra 10'-8" increase in the main room (and overall house length) significantly enhances the main living zoom, yet the total plan is still under 1,200 sq.ft. total. Several key highlights of the larger ranch are:

MAXI ranch highlights (see fig. 4.6):

- 1,173 sq.ft. total (20'×58'-10" footprint), 8 timber trusses
- 2 bedroom, 2 bath layout
- Great room = 640 sq.ft. (20'×32;), 5 timber trusses
- Master bedroom = 205 sq.ft. (16'×21'-10"),

2 timber trusses
- Guest bedroom = 127 sq.ft. (10'-8"×11'-10" entry), 1 timber truss
- Master bath = 64 sq.ft.
- Master closet = 52 sq.ft.
- Guest bath = 62 sq.ft.
- Guest bedroom closet = 11 sq.ft.

The MAXI ranch in/out ratio:

- Total exterior wall length = 158 linear feet
- Total interior wall length = 86 linear feet
- In/out ratio = 55%

Thus, the MAXI is even "more open" that then MINI ranch!

ALTERNATE COAT CLOSET/PANTRY: COMPUTER NOOK

An optional layout to the dual coat closet and pantry alcoves between the rear entry door and the kitchen along the north wall can be achieved fairly simply. This alternative floor plan can trade off the two alcoves between the two timber truss spaced 64" zones to gain a mini office. See fig. 4.7, page 77 for details.

Essentially we are increasing the area out from the wall several inches and combining the coat sections and the pantry into one alcove. The pantry 10" shelves, nearer the kitchen, can line that wall from floor to the 7' height where the utility chase goes through the closet area. The 2' depth needed for the coats is on the side nearer the entry door and now the computer nook alcove. By freeing up the zone closer to the entry door, we can make a computer nook.

Note that using the vertical 4×4 and 4×6 pine posts to interface to the similar matching timber trusses, the 2×8 T&G pine decking used for the roof, can be notched into the sides/front of these alcoves for walls. Thus, a simple/thinner, yet structural wall, results without the thickness and complexity of 2×4 studs and the multiple *Sheetrock* layers.

COMPUTER NOOK FEATURES:

- Small triangular computer desk can fit in adjacent to the coat side of the T&G dividing wall (T&G notches on computer nook side)
- 2-shelf file cabinet can fit in opposite corner (about 28" tall, and 15", 18", or 22" depth, etc.)
- Short file cabinet should be adequate for small computer printer location
- 15"W×10"L-deep bookcase can fit into middle of the nook's back wall
- Even more shelves can be added on the two T&G alcove structural walls (no wall anchors needed)
- Key feature: Removes the home office needs from impacting the second bedroom resulting in unique zone on its own.

SUMMARY OF MAXI RANCH

In general, I believe a significant number of seriously intended "downsizing- retirees" should find this almost 1,200 sq.ft. MAXI ranch a neat home for the retirement years. Check again the Figure 4.5 dramatic image of the similar 5-truss great room. And yet, we have a modest sized, relatively simple, and structurally superior home in play. The owners should feel more than just downsized!

If a client has a larger budget for a more elaborate floor plan with more space needs, another home shape, with similar quality construction traits as just discussed, follows in Chapter 5.

Figure 4.5 Multiple-truss great room example (really a ranch?).

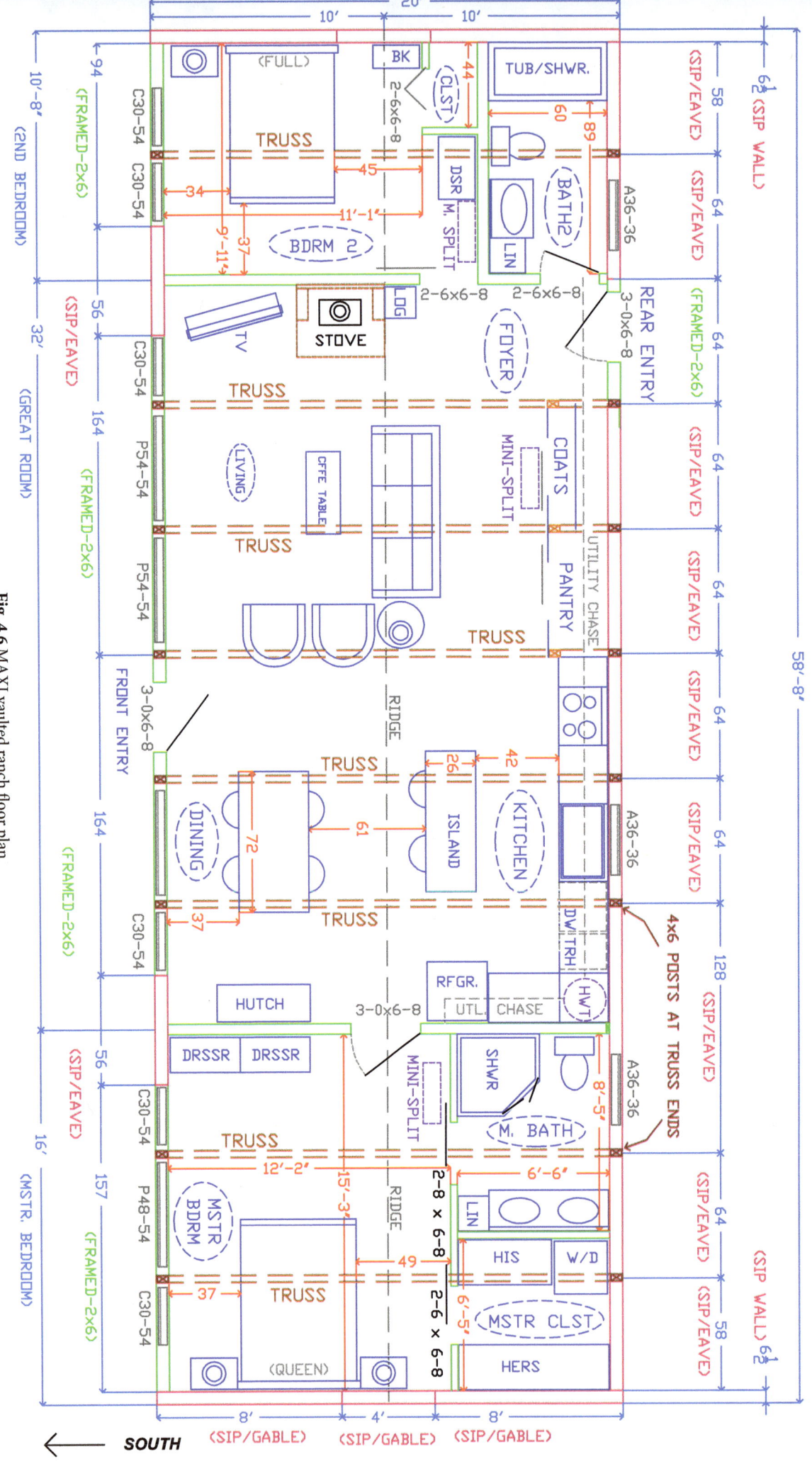

Fig. 4.6 MAXI vaulted ranch floor plan

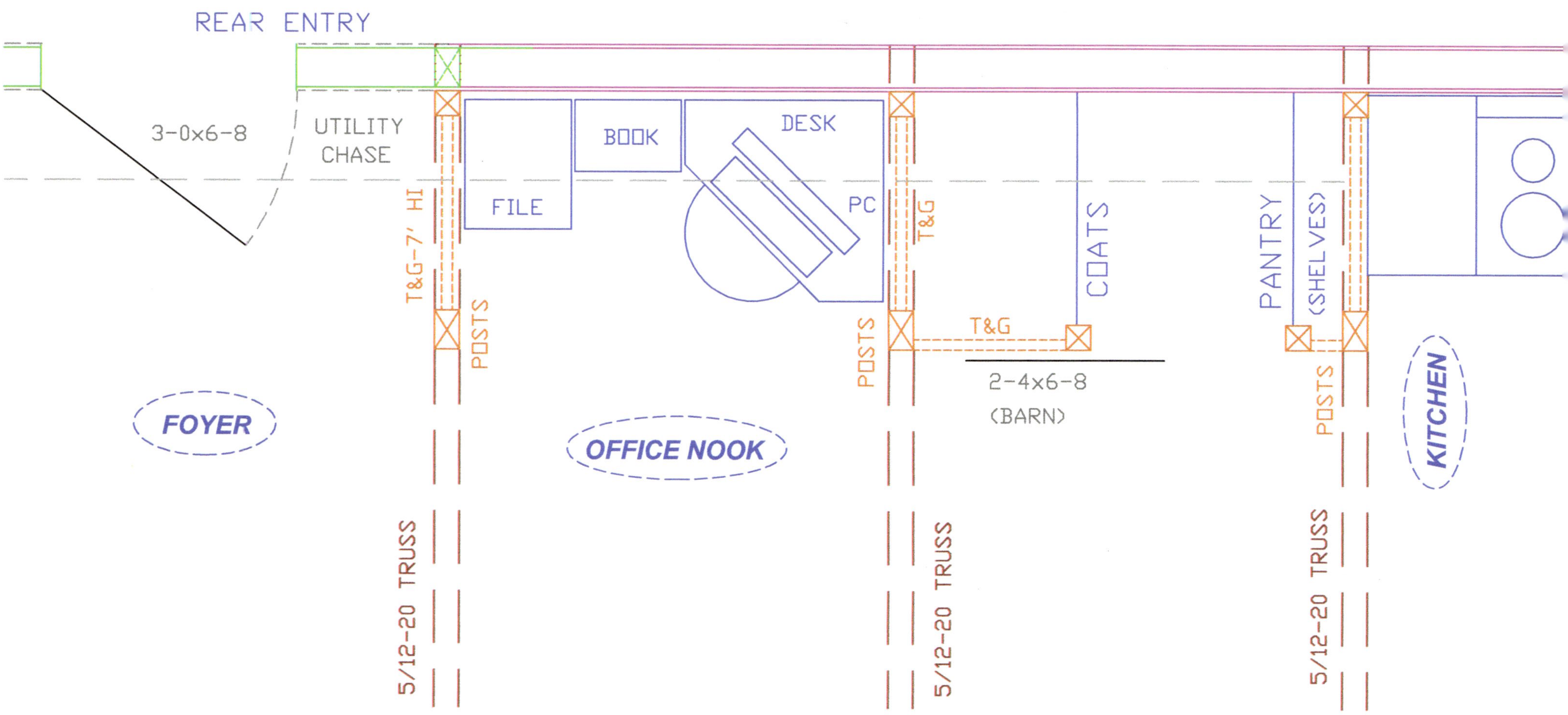

Fig. 4.7 Computer nook (alternate pantry/coats)

chapter five

Tee chalet

With the most basic shape (ranches) just covered, we can move up slightly in complexity to the TEE (T) shape. By using two smaller ranch-like, partial house modules, more sophistication results. Also, on some building lots, the T-shape may actually fit into property terrain as well as enabling some unique options for privacy with neighboring houses.

After noting the general shape of this plan the TEE portion of the title is evident. The Chalet part is partially buried in the description of all of our house types here. That is, all the Cathedral Ranches discussed here are similar to the Mountain Chalet's discussed in Chapter 2. The major difference just exemplified in the Figure 3.17 is our 5/12 roof pitch, which is more modest than the typical 12/12 steep mountain cabin roof. Those cabins usually acquire the Chalet label. Our chalets are similarly vaulted, with exposed ceilings, but are more practical.

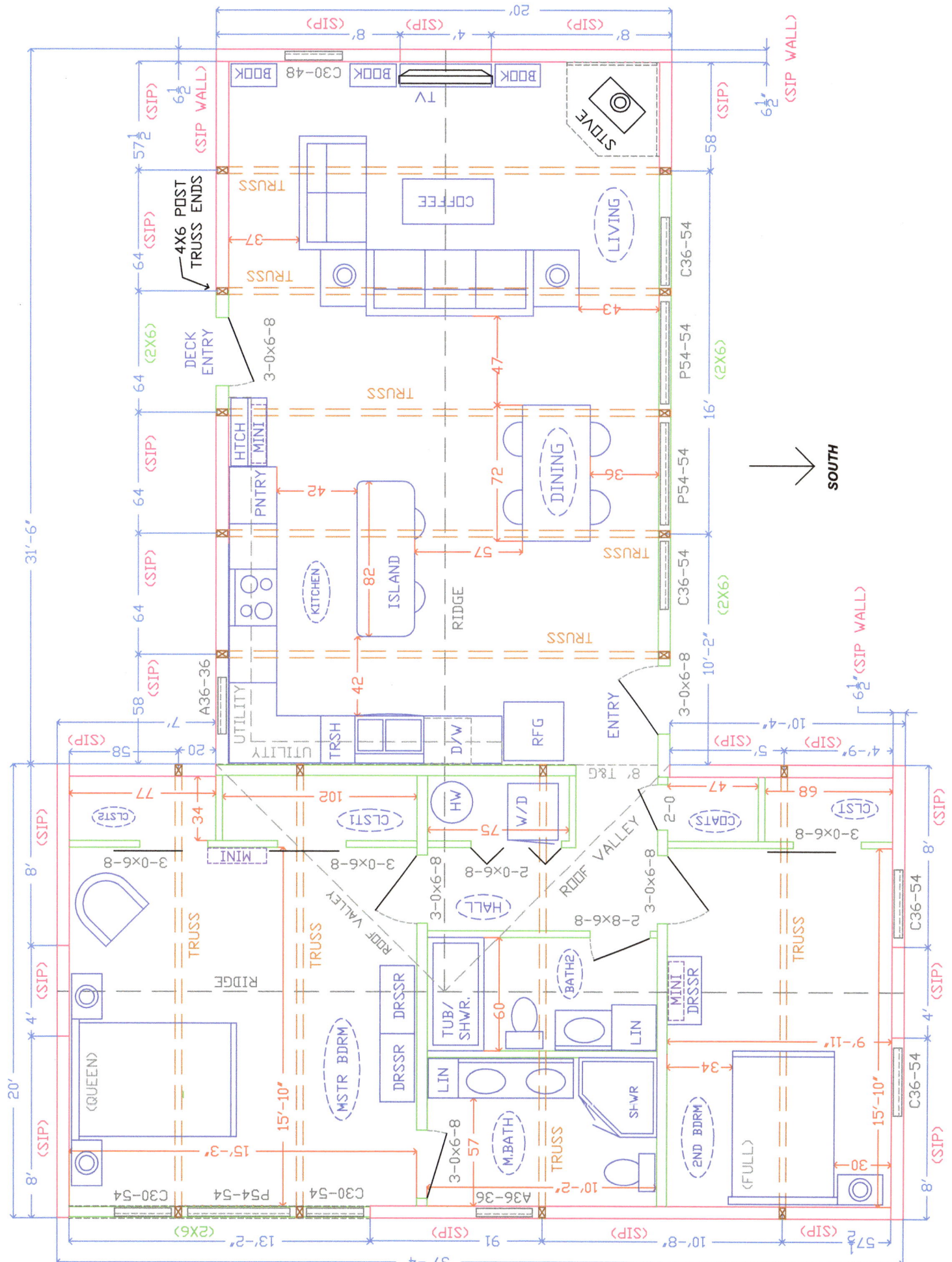

Figure 5.1 TEE chalet floor plan

The following elevation drawing (prominent south side view) in Figure 5.2 demonstrates that the bedroom wing gable points to the view side on the left with the ranch-like Great Room module on the right side.

EXAMPLE OF T-SHAPED HOME

A picture of this T-shaped entry zone in a similar Timber Truss homes follows in figure 5.3. This SIP-based home utilized the taller 8/12-20', *Glulam*-based trusses, similar to the earlier Fig. 1.2 Great Room. This Great Room used the 64"-spaced-trusses so the resulting 32'-long living module is the identical size as the Figure 5.1 plan footprint.

Note this home filled in the front inside corner of the T-shape for a very large entry porch. (They also have a large rear porch.) Note also that this frequently desired feature will darken the inside of the home. And if one desires to take advantage of passive solar, energy-gain enhancement, trading the total porch roof area back to an uncovered deck or patio is a key factor to weigh. By the way, the large SIP gable section picture on this front cover is from this actual home.

One may note the exterior top section of the protruding gable with decorative "shingle" siding also indicates the extra wall area (and inside ceiling height) of the 8/12-pitched roof profile here. The 5/12 simpler trusses we utilize for these plans is about 3' less steep ridge peak. Or about 71sq.ft. for the 8/12s and about 50sq.ft. for the lower 5/12's = 21sq.ft. less wall area per gable than the steeper version. This means everywhere a tall gable wall exists in the home, both interior or exterior, this 21sq.ft. number multiplies. It also highlights that in addition to the actual material increase, you have exterior finishes (like the fancy "shingle" in the upper gable Figure 5.3 picture and the interior, likely *Sheetrock*, increases in area. Note again that the "roof run" numbers in the Figure 3.17 comparison of the extreme 12/12 pitch and the utilized here 5/12 pitch also compounds the costs (but at the mid-level 8/12 rate in the picture) so, the reader can now begin to understand that this really does expand the overall home construction costs.

MODULARITY AT WORK

Since we strive to use the useful building blocks (our "Modules") throughout, we only need to address the few differences on this more complex-than-ranch house. The most significant point of utilizing two very large, each about one-half house, modules joined together at the 90° intersection, yields two significant property-site-related factors:

1. The slightly more complex "T" adds more interesting appearance than the basic ranch.
2. The inside two corners formed by the T enables front and rear porch/decks that could enable more private nooks (especially important in smaller building lots with side houses closer).

The two large sub-house sections are the familiar Great Room section (looks very similar truss pattern I Figure 4.5) and the bedroom wing.

Since most of the two main modules and building technologies are very similar to the Ranches, we will only highlight the major differences.

ROOF VALLEY FRAMING NOTES:

The most significant external structural feature and key difference to the simpler ranches is that we now have to add a "Roof Valley" section at the intersection of the two large modules. This is a "traditional framed" section to mate the two 5/12 roofs coming together. Key points are:

1. Framed in with 2×6 rafters after the full roof "sandwich" is complete on both modules.
2. Horizontal nailer 2×6 plates on the top CDX plywood sandwich roof use longer panel screws to secure to inner 2×8 roof decking.
3. A simple 2×12 or LVL ridge beam fills in the 10' gap between the bedroom and Great Room module ridges. The rafters attach from the new ridge extension down to the nailer on the completed roofs.
4. CDX top plywood sheathing nailed on hand-framed rafters (16" on center).
5. Ice/water shield membrane is on the entire

FIGURE 5.2 – Tee Chalet south elevation

FIGURE 5.3 – Example T shape entry side elevation view

valley section
6. Spray foam (minimum R30) sprayed on raters after completion.
7. Best access to zone is access door (24"× 30") in gable end at bedroom closet and kitchen
8. See fig. 5.2 also

MISCELLANEOUS CONSTRUCTION NOTES:

- The shared gable wall at the kitchen juncture with the bedroom module fits the more practical scheme of 2×6 framing, and not SIP!
- The plumbing and wiring access needs at this juncture wall is very significant
- The internal side of the kitchen need the layer of OSB sheathing
- However, in this case, due to closets on the back side of the kitchen gable framed wall, the two eave wall "wings" out from the kitchen gable can be SIPs. No wiring is needed in the closets on those SIP walls means simplifying wiring.
- However, the second layer of 7/16" OSB is not needed to match with SIP wall thickness because we choose to add the mid-wall between to form two master closets, his and hers for two size choices
- The long Great Room south framed window wall (with 4 windows) can be broken down into two framed sub-modules as shown or go with a longer special order 20' plates for all the windows in the framed module and only the entry door section framed in last at the building site
- All of these pre-framed modules, including the internal 2×6 and smaller 2×4 walls can be shop framed and brought to the site with a reasonable trailer size (18-20' deck-over style)
- The area composed of the second bath, the hall, and the washer/dryer room will work nicely as an 8' flat ceiling with the same 2×8 T&G. Since the spans are reasonable, like on the main roof, just the T&G nailed across the 8' walls. The same 16' long T&G will simply span that area. This eliminates most the roof wall extension to the ceiling, except in the Master Bath. The resulting loft above the already structural T&G decking also is very useful storage space (access hatch in hall of washer/dryer room in flat ceiling T&G.). I strongly advise multiple coats of water-based urethane on the second bathroom T&G underside though. Also, part of the loft can be used as utility zones for ducting, wiring, and even some water line routing.

GREAT ROOM FEATURES:

- The kitchen area is nestled in the corner forming a very useful sized L pattern with the Island bar counter centrally located
- The utility chase scheme is highly advised here, but is on both walls that form the kitchen wide L. The indoor mini-split can again mount on the utility chase side near the middle of the long Great Room area (at the end of the north utility chase).
- The living portion is focused on the opposite end from the kitchen zone with the TV/Stove/Window triad more focused on the exterior gable wall
- The resulting zone midway between the kitchen and the living/seating area, but offset to non-kitchen eave wall enables the dining table to move closer to the window eave wall (likely South?)
- The shared gable wall of the kitchen to the now separate washer/dryer nook enables much of the plumbing to be concentrated near the two bathrooms also.
- The 4-window scheme yields about 14 linear feet of window on this prominent south wall. (Far above the typical suburban "parlor" or living room in the average Atlanta 1960-1980 suburban split levels plans where 6-9' of width is typical)

MASTER BEDROOM FEATURES:

- The different room layout takes advantage of two master closets (his and hers) on eave side near the kitchen gable wall.
- The opposite gable wall then enables our typical 3-window scheme located between

the Timber Trusses
- The Master bathroom then forms a slightly different footprint than the more space efficient dual-side row scheme we employed in the smaller ranches.
- The Master's 3-window is shown on the west eave wall Vs the typical gable end wall, providing a different house side location, if the property can take advantage of that side.

GUEST BEDROOM FEATURES:

- The long, narrow, single-truss bedroom module now enables space at one end for its closet zone
- The other zone, with access to the internal hall area, provides space for a Coat Closet
- Important to note that the space needed to connect the kitchen, Master Bedroom, and the second bedroom is now beginning to use up some of the larger square footage budget of this plan over the basic ranches (where space efficiency is a premium there). Essentially, we are paying a little more for the more enhanced floor plan here.
- The Guest bathroom does position a good balance in location to the second bedroom and to the public areas.

WINDOW SIZING OPTIONS

The reader may note on the floor plan window text that the two flanking casement windows are the wider 36" Vs the smaller homes using the typical 30" width. Two factors are related to this width increase:

1. Since we have less window potential on this south Great Room wall here in the T layout (only 4 between-truss zones) because the corner zone near the exterior gable end is a solid wall for the wood stove. Thus the extra window width is a good upgrade for the other four between-truss spots we do have.
2. The wider window just adds to the energy gain and daylighting factor of the Great Room if the owner chooses to enable Passive Solar gain.

Note also that the Master's 3-window scheme could also be shifted to the north (tall SIP gable wall) instead of the shown west wall version (if near neighbor privacy on the west is an issue at the specific site). Also, the window shift to the north wall if a preferred view is there. (But, at more energy loss in colder months.)

Another variation of the window sizing can play out in the right side of the elevation view of the Guest bedroom. As the plan notes, since this is the Guest, or second bedroom, we chose not to show the preferred Triple-window scheme we typically have in the Master bedroom. We do have the two wider 36" casements shown though. The owner can upgrade the smaller bedroom also to the triple scheme if they prefer for the increased costs (the extra 54"× 54" picture window). Again, this enhancement is more relevant if Passive Solar is in play since in this T plan, the Master bedroom, is on the back of the house and not on the typical South side.

T-SHAPED INTERIOR PICTURES

The next two Figures, 5.4 and 5.5 will aid the reader visually on how some of the more practical variations of merging the Timber Truss and SIP wall construction technologies have progressed with the simpler, lower cost 5/12-20' pine trusses.

FIGURE 5.4
- Earlier project used 8/12-20' trusses in simpler "King" style
- Total Great Room length = 32' with this 64" truss spacing
- Note left wall has only triple window pattern (our T here has extra 54"-wide picture unit)
- This large panel SIP version did have buried dual studs at the truss ends (new plans use smaller 64"-wide with 4×6 posts at junctions)
- The steeper 8/12 pitch does indicate the extra gable end material required over the current 5/12s

IN/OUT RATIO

To check how "open" this T plan really is, we utilize our IN/OUT ratio scheme with the following data:
- Exterior walls = 178 linear feet
- Interior walls = 121 linear feet
- IN/OUT RATIO = 68%

Thus, the T is still relatively open plan, but the more complex walls needed to make the layout flow is starting to add to the total wall distances and thus the cost increases associated there. Please glance back at the "Maxi" ranch figures to now appreciate how "efficient" that floor plan is!

TEE PLAN WRAP UP

The key summary of this more sophisticated layout is that we now have a small luxury upgrade due to more square footage in all the major zones of the house. For example, the Master bedroom is about 264 sq.ft. vs. the bigger ranch at 205 sq.ft. The guest bedroom moves from 127 sq.ft. to a very respectable 176 sq.ft. The Great room is almost identical to the bigger ranch since that space was already a top asset. (Review Figure 1.3 for all specifics.)

Now we can take another step in floor plan complexity in the next chapter.

FIGURE 5.5
- Kitchen L view in earlier SIP project in T-shaped home similar to our newer T
- Earlier project also used steeper 8/12-20' trusses in simpler "King" style
- Total Great Room length = 36'- long with the wider 72" truss spacing (not used in newer plans)
- This Kitchen did use the taller 8' high cabinets and not the 12" utility chase we suggest
- Since this project had a basement with engineered floor trusses, utility runs were naturally located there
- Our newer, simpler, slab foundations homes we now employ, the above-cabinet (7' off floor) utility chase version does streamline the construction process
- 8'-tall cabinets actually too high to reach, without steps tool, particularly for aging clients
- Our newer L kitchen is actually wider than this 1,700 sq. ft. home and the newer bar/counter/island position is rotated 90°

chapter six

The winged chalet

The winged tag on this new floor plan style is due to the location of the two bedrooms. They are on both sides of the central Great Room (our now, four-truss module on this smaller, first of two versions). Thus, the bedrooms are outlying "wings" to the centered Great Room. The fundamental difference here with the Great Room now is that it is 90° from our earlier pattern such that the 20' gable end wall becomes prominent for the street view. Note that this requires more floor plan design diligence to gain enough window area on this wall as the four small "bump-outs" due to the now 26'-8" long Great Room section extending past the 20' bedroom wing widths. This shape was very much utilized in my earlier work, *Building Today's Green Home*, as in the picture above.

The resulting South elevation, or likely "street view," is shown in fig. 6.1 (see facing page).

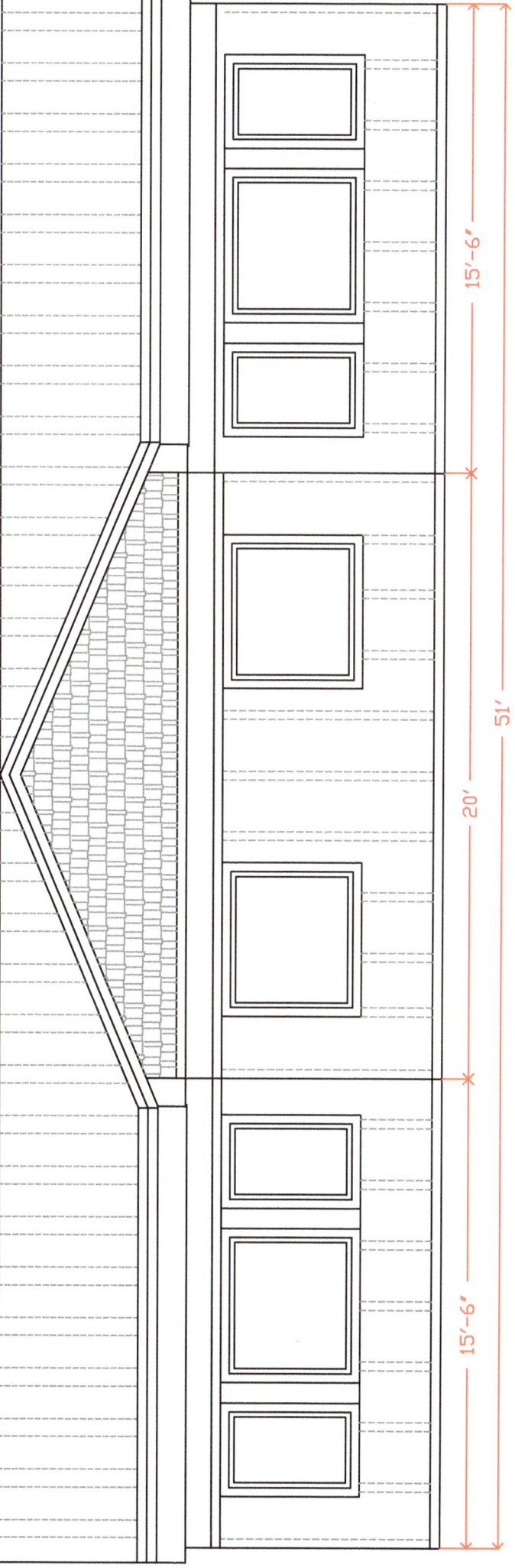

Fig. 6.1 Street view elevation of Winged Chalet 2-bedroom version

The gable end of the middle 20' of the house bump-outs from the principal longer left-to-right length of the building. Since the entry door is on the right short side of this bump-out, it can't be seen in this view (see fig. 6.1 on previous page). The two most general points of this plan beyond the protruding gable is that both the bedroom "wings" on either side are the same and this "crossing" pattern of the two house macro modules now form two sets of roof valley in-fill framing sections. (The same as in the past chapter "TEE" only had one pair.)

Before moving on to a more extensive review of the floor plan review from fig. 6.3, fig. 6.2 (see below) illustrates the valley-infill framing module details. This picture is actually during the construction of "The Walnut Mountain" *EnergyStar* project house from my earlier book, *Building Today's Green Home*.

Note: Only the main floor is shown in fig. 6.3 here as a basement foundation is needed on this steep mountain lot.

Fig. 6.2 Roof valley infill framing example

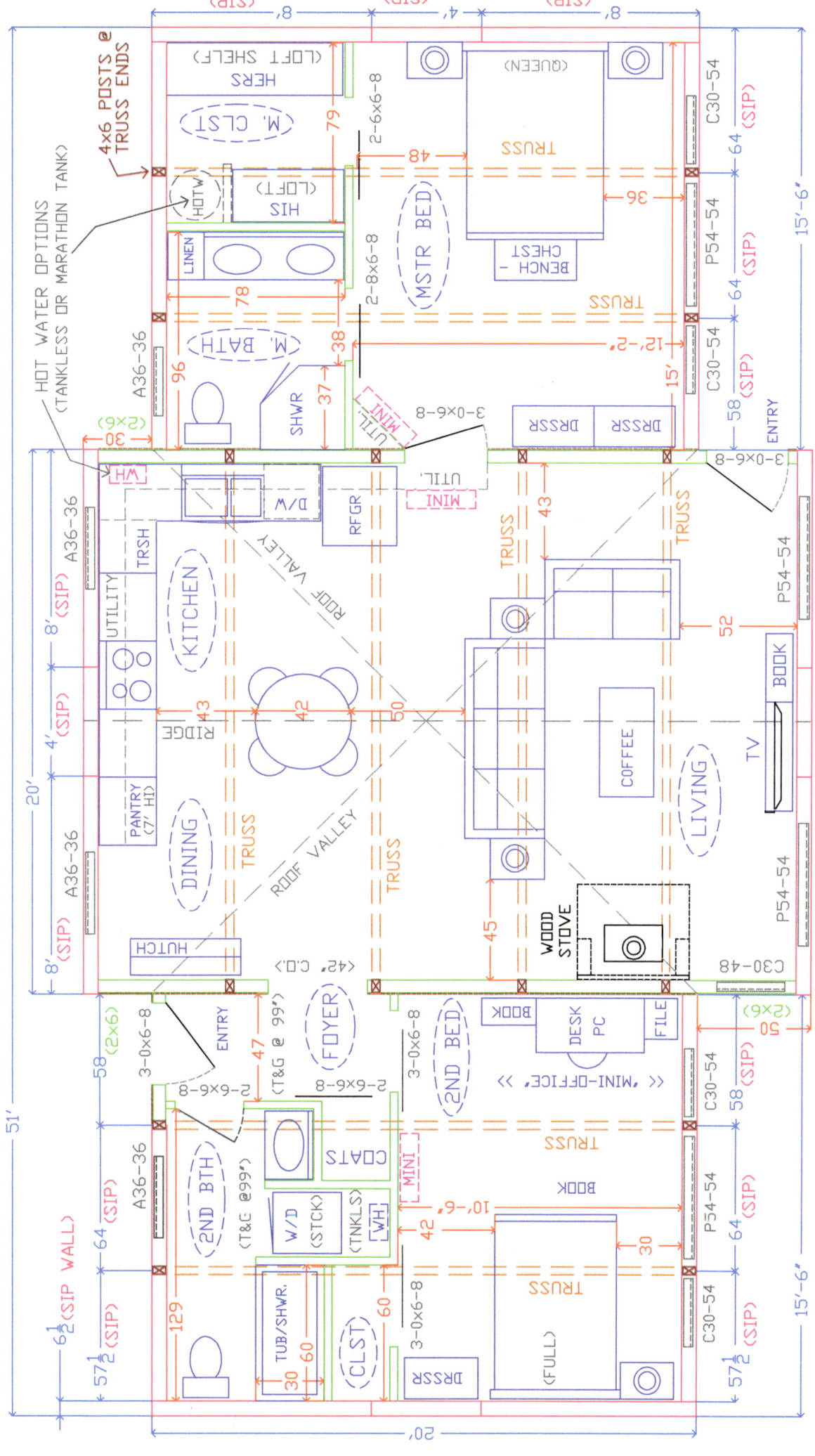

Fig. 6.3 Floor plan of "Winged" Chalet 2-bedroom version

FLOOR PLAN HIGHLIGHTS:

Great Room

- Most significant is that the Great room now is only 4 Timber Trusses, netting a 26'-8" long room by 20' = 533 sq.ft.**
- The protruding gable bump-out does yield two 54" × 54" picture windows
- Note: maxi ranch has three picture windows, plus an extra c30"× 54" casement.
- A smaller c30"× 48" casement on the left bump out side is for a ventilating window
- Should still be an egress-opening rated unit in quality window brands, like *Jeld-Wenn*
- Entry door on the right bump-out side
- Wood stove near left corner affords a reasonable view but the central TV and the two picture windows are the most prominent features
- The seating is roughly centered mid-way under the two Timber Trusses, fairly dramatic seating plus the lighting/fan features can be added easily with some secondary wood beams there

**Note: The 533 sq.ft. Great room area still compares fairly well to the typical mountain cabins in our region, have 24'×24' zones = 576 sq.ft., thus we are only 7% less in the smaller of two plans in this chapter.

Kitchen

- The slightly smaller space with just four trusses does show up in the Kitchen layout since we still have a nice wide "L" counter layout, but
- Trying to squeeze in an Island and/or a very large family-size rectangular table would be too much crowding (for retired couple here, remember, not a growing full family!)
- The utility chase is best used in both sides of the L-layout, with the mini-slit HVAC unit positioned nicely around mid-room, (note: likely dual system here for great room and Master bedroom only)
- Note that two of the A36"×36" awning windows can be positioned on the kitchen gable exterior wall and still have room for a hutch for dishes, etc. cabinet near the left awning
- Choice of tankless water heater can be put in the dead corner of the base cabinets

Dining room

- The best fitting 42"-round dining table is shown. With the chairs at 45°, then their movement into the walk zones is not as impactful as a rectangular 3'× 5' table would be
- The central table zone in the middle of the two back Timber Trusses is a pretty dramatic placement also
- The hutch location, if willing to forgo that piece of furniture, could yield a "mini-office" desk zone . . . but note the second bedroom version below first

Master Bedroom

- The overall shape of this master is identical to the Maxi-Ranch from Chapter 4.
- But, for reference, I shown the larger sized, "tanked" Marathon long-life, hot water heater (vs the Tankless version that can fit in the kitchen corner base) in the closet in this version layout.
- Since we have a spot in the larger second bedroom wing, I show the stacked Washer/Dryer configuration there in this version (I prefer in the Master Closet, though)

Second Bedroom

- The most significant feature is the jump in total area (now 174 sq.ft.) available for the second bedroom as well as the bath and closet needs there over the smaller Ranch's
- There is also a nice closet-size increase over the ranches
- Most significant: The large second bedroom enables a decent "mini-office" zone against the shared Great Room wall and near the right casement window. In lieu of a third bedroom, this is a good solution for the total house square footage here

- The overall bathroom size is fine, but dividing up all the zones with the stacked washer/dryer spot does add more wall framing

Ceiling note for Second Bathroom Hall:

- As we discussed in the last chapter with the "TEE", we recommended using a flat ceiling in the hallway, 2nd bath, second closet, etc.
- This is implemented again with the same 2×8 T&G roof decking from the main roof
- The T&G is nailed directly over the, now 99"-high top plates and 2×4 horizontal nailers in the SIP wall zones (8" SIP panel screw from outside into horizontal nailer, cover with 1×4 and 1×3 trim on finishing)
- This eliminates most of the wall vertical extensions to the vaulted ceiling except in the one second bedroom wall (where access hatch could be installed to the loft area now formed)

In/Out Ratio

To check how "open" this smaller winged-chalet plan really compares to the earlier plan types, we again apply our in/out ratio scheme with the following data:
- Exterior walls = 155 linear feet
- Interior walls = 106 linear feet
- In/Out ratio = 68%

This smaller winged chalet is relatively open, despite the second bath zones and two of the internal walls forming the Great Room eaves. It almost has an exterior structural function due to the crossing pattern of the large house sections.

Larger Winged Chalet #3

To provide some slightly larger home options, we will discuss the first of two 3-bedroom versions now: The Winged Chalet #3 title is implying the bedroom quantity. The street view is very similar to the smaller model with the principal feature due to the adding of this third bedroom. Thus, the left side "wing" with both the 2nd and 3rd bedrooms is distinctly wider in the following Fig. 6.4 now than the also extended Master bedroom section. (Houses don't always have to be perfectly "symmetrical"!)

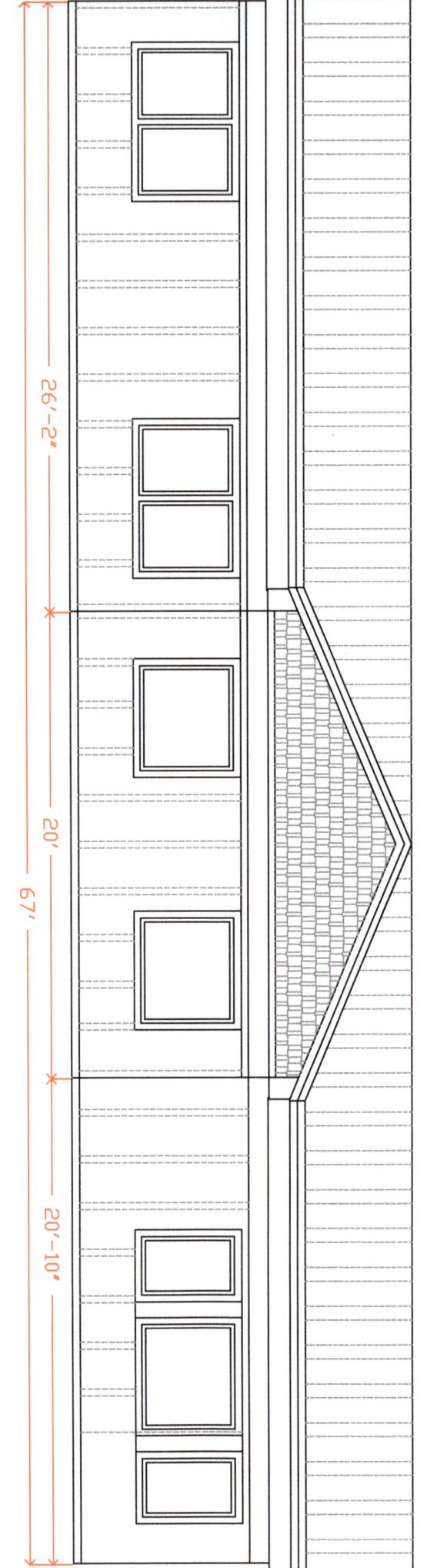

Fig. 6.4 Street view elevation of "Winged" Chalet 3-bedroom version

GENERAL ELEV. OBSERVATIONS:

In addition to the asymmetric sizing, a few other key points can be noted from the main elevation view:

1. The standard protruding Great room gable wall has the two nice size "Picture" windows (noted as P54"× 54" = 54"-wide and 54"-high, non venting, fixed glass)
2. Both bedroom windows, due to single Timber Truss dictated width of 10'-8" have a pair of "Casement" windows (C36"-54"). Note though that these are the wider 36" versions
3. The Master bedroom wing on the right has only typical "triple window" scheme with the centered 54" picture unit and the two 30"-wide flanking, venting type casements
4. The Great room upper gable zone is a good place for a mild cosmetic upgrade as in the shingles shown

MISC. CONSTRUCTION NOTES:

- In general, more internal walls are needed to obtain more zones and connecting hallways
- The mid-located Great room is now back up to our five-truss version with the nice 32'-long layout very useful here
- The extra 64" framed, not Timber Truss, zone in the master bedroom wing to obtain closet space is pretty evident, (resulting in two spots – one hers and one his)
- A similar two-gable framed wall pair is utilized in the 2nd/3rd bedroom wing to gain both closet and second bathroom areas
- This large area in the 2nd/3rd wing, including the hallway from the foyer to the bedroom doors is another good place to utilize the flat pine T&G structural technique (at our 99"-high top plate height). This results in both a utility chase zone and much needed storage lofts above while eliminating most of the vertical extensions from the flat ceiling to the vaulted one
- The second bedroom closet is best to do the elevated walls and use this extra vaulted zone for much taller shelves (for overflow boxes?) in either end of this narrow, dual ended layout

FLOOR PLAN HIGHLIGHTS:

Great Room

- The Great Room with the five timber trussed, 32'-long room (640 sq. ft.) is again impressive
- The longer room makes the "Living/seating" zone grouped in the gable bump-out area with two "picture" 54" × 54" windows, a wood stove, a TV zone, and side venting casement window all meshing well together
- The general flow of the entire Great Room now even meshes well with the three sub-zones (Kitchen, dining and living) and in general, does not feel crowded

Kitchen

- The kitchen "L" shape works nicely again here with the added, long, narrow island bar/counter blending in
- The utility chase in the L- layout also functions well aiding the Great Room indoor Mini-split unit located near mid-room (and aids in some of the Master bath needs = exhaust fan duct?).
- The two larger A36"× 36" awning windows on the rear bump-out gable wall is a general upgrade
- The tall "pantry" cabinet can also be wider here for more kitchen supplies
- The corner zone near the left 3'× 3' awning window could be an extra "desk" location to complement the upcoming spot in the 2nd bedroom (now two distinct desk locations?)

Dining

- The dining table can grow to at least a 6' rectangle shape with ample chair movement spots
- The central table located directly under two Timber Trusses is dramatic

- The "Hutch" dish type cabinet can now fit near the dining table and refrigerator spots

Master Bedroom

- The master's square footage has increased back close to the earlier Tee Chalet version (now 256 sq. ft.)
- We have again, my preferred triple-window scheme
- The master bath is now a long, narrow layout with functions on both ends and the window in the middle (and uses the full vaulted ceiling)
- The master closet is now a two-section affair with the likely "Hers" labeled unit being larger

2nd Bedroom

- The total area is a solid 170 sq. ft. with the 3rd bedroom space now also available
- The dual casement windows are the larger 36"-wide version
- A respectable desk spot near the closet is a practical utilization
- The dual-ended closet with the vaulted extra, "mini-loft, higher shelves," adds more storage space

Foyer/Hallway

- The foyer is best left vaulted here and focuses the view on part of the Timber Truss there on entering the home, which will likely be the normal daily entry-use door
- The hallway now provides two key spots to be the Coat closet and a side-by-side Washer/Dryer niche (if needs are more oriented to this side of the house)
- A tankless water heater could fit in either of the two above zones.

2nd Bathroom

- The bathroom layout is the typical "compact apartment" size, about 5' wide × 8' long. But, the typical 30"× 60" tub implies the two gable walls need to go to 2×4, which is okay, or the preferred 2×6 versions offset 1-1/2" to fit, or one end of the tub has just a portion with 2×4 studs
- The flat ceiling here (at 99") also aids in the exhaust fan duct exiting from this mid-house location.
- The pine T&G ceiling needs multiple water-based urethane coating for moisture protection

3rd Bedroom

- The area, as expected, drops from the 2nd unit's size, and a realistic bed size is thus necessary
- A better fit for this room is the focus more on a Hobby/Craft/office, with maybe a small pull-out futon type bed as the extra guest bed spot
- With the two other potential "desk zones" already discussed for a couple's needs, the emphasis on this zone now being more a Craft/Hobby space, than a guest bedroom, is more achievable

In/Out Ratio

As alluded to in the construction notes, we suspect the In/Out ratio will be changing. Thus when applying the following data we have:

- Exterior walls = 198 linear feet
- Interior walls = 187 linear feet
- In/Out ratio = 95%

Thus, the numbers confirm the pattern we noted earlier. In fact the total exterior wall amount is also growing in addition to the interior walls, implying the cost per sq. ft. will increase even more. Note that we still have the "OPEN" Great Room technique in the middle of the home.

And now we will move on to the largest floor plan of this exercise in chapter 7.

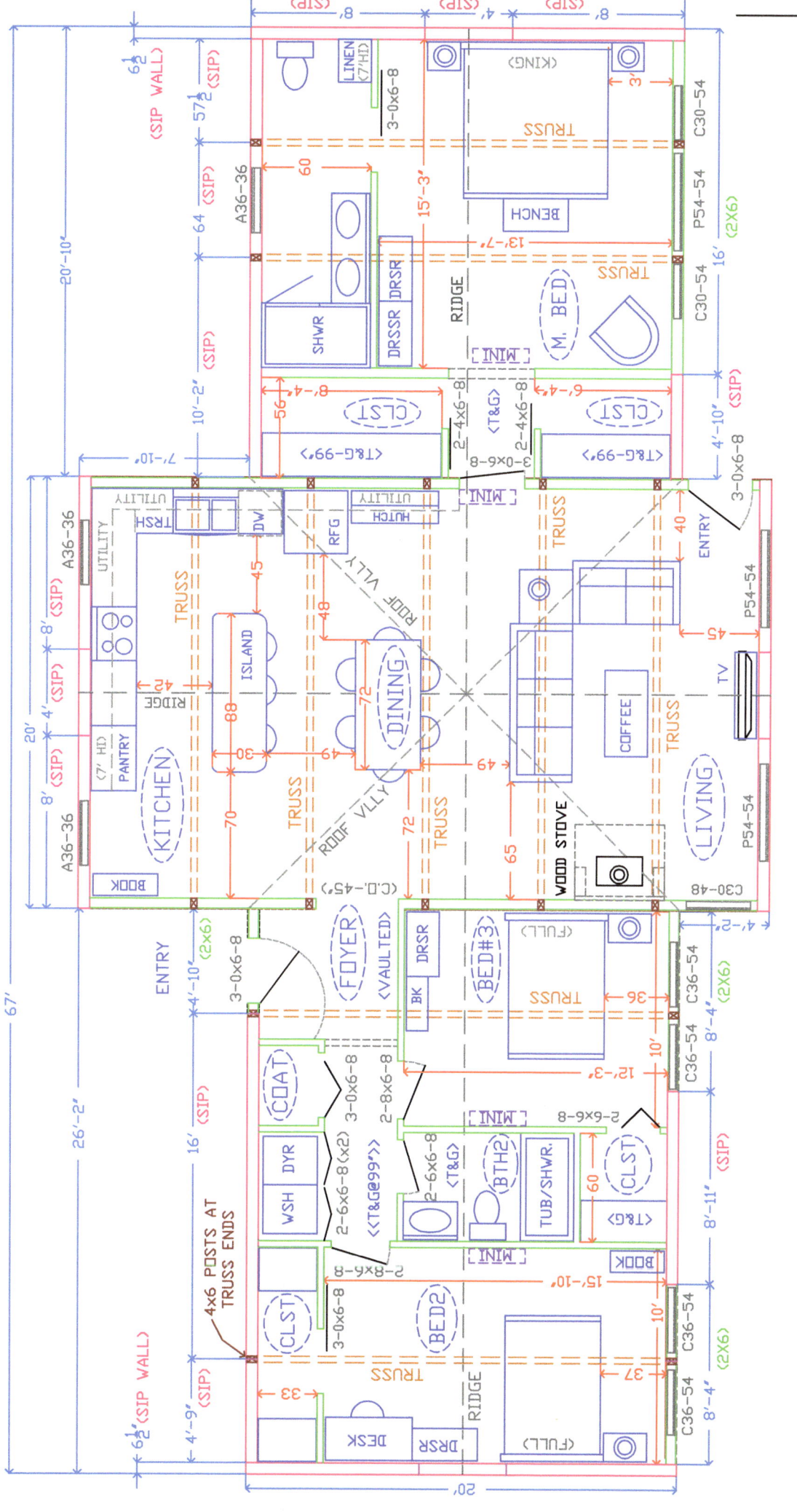

Fig. 6.5 Floor plan of "Winged" Chalet 3-bedroom version

Fig. 7.1 Picture of typical street view of Squashed-H

chapter seven

The "Squashed-H"

The reader is likely wondering about our "labelling" many of these plans with some alphabetical link! But the letter "H" is so well a fit, it must be employed here. The "Squashed" part implies the two Bedroom "wings" on either side of the central, now standard, 32'-long Great Room module, are much shorter than seen in the TEE shaped versions. The Great Room run runs horizontally left-to-right, like a ranch, but unlike in the winged chalets just discussed, Those two shorter wings produce the dual-gable street view often seen in many American neighborhoods. This is quite apparent in the above fig. 7.1 street view picture. Again, just two protruding gables, not nineteen! (Note this is the slightly larger version using the larger timber trusses at the wider 72" spacing with the Great Room 4' longer). The matching elevation view drawing is in fig. 7.2

The two gables are quite prominent is this typical street view. Note the gables with the triple-window pattern have the extended window, sun-shading, "overhangs" for this Passive Solar house. (Note the late September, midday sunline beginning to enter into the windows in the three South wall window zones.) A custom metal awing for the two gables and the smaller entry porch could be a visual upgrade if the budget is available.

Importantly note that the typical real estate "curb-appeal first, sales mentality" is to add a huge entry porch in this view. That would cancel out the Passive Solar boost and Great Room daylighting advantages of our approach.

With that perspective, we can look at the actual floor plan details in Figure 7.3

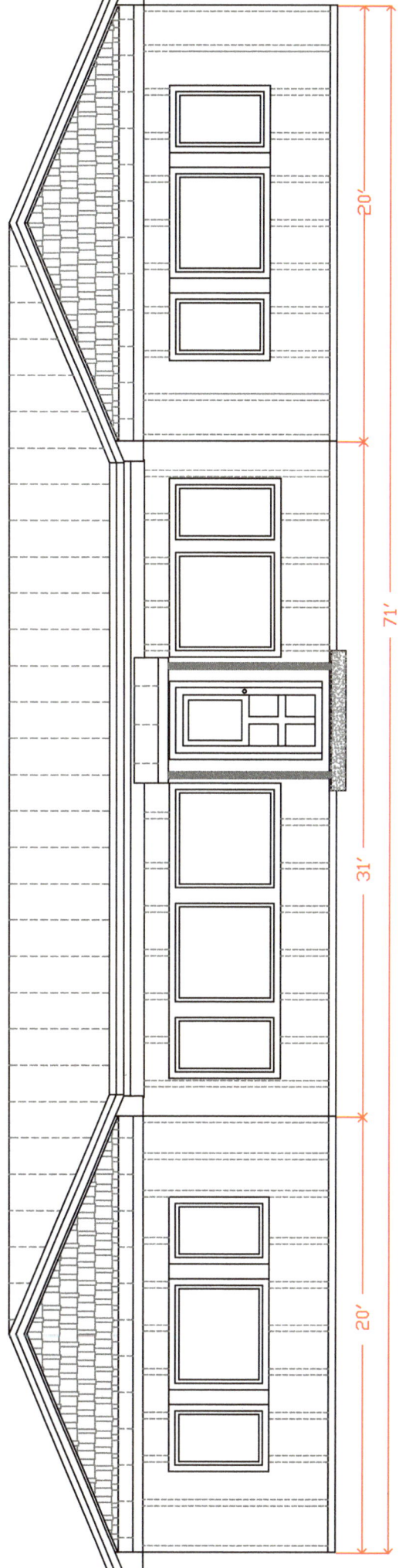

Fig. 7.2 South elevation view of Squashed-H plan

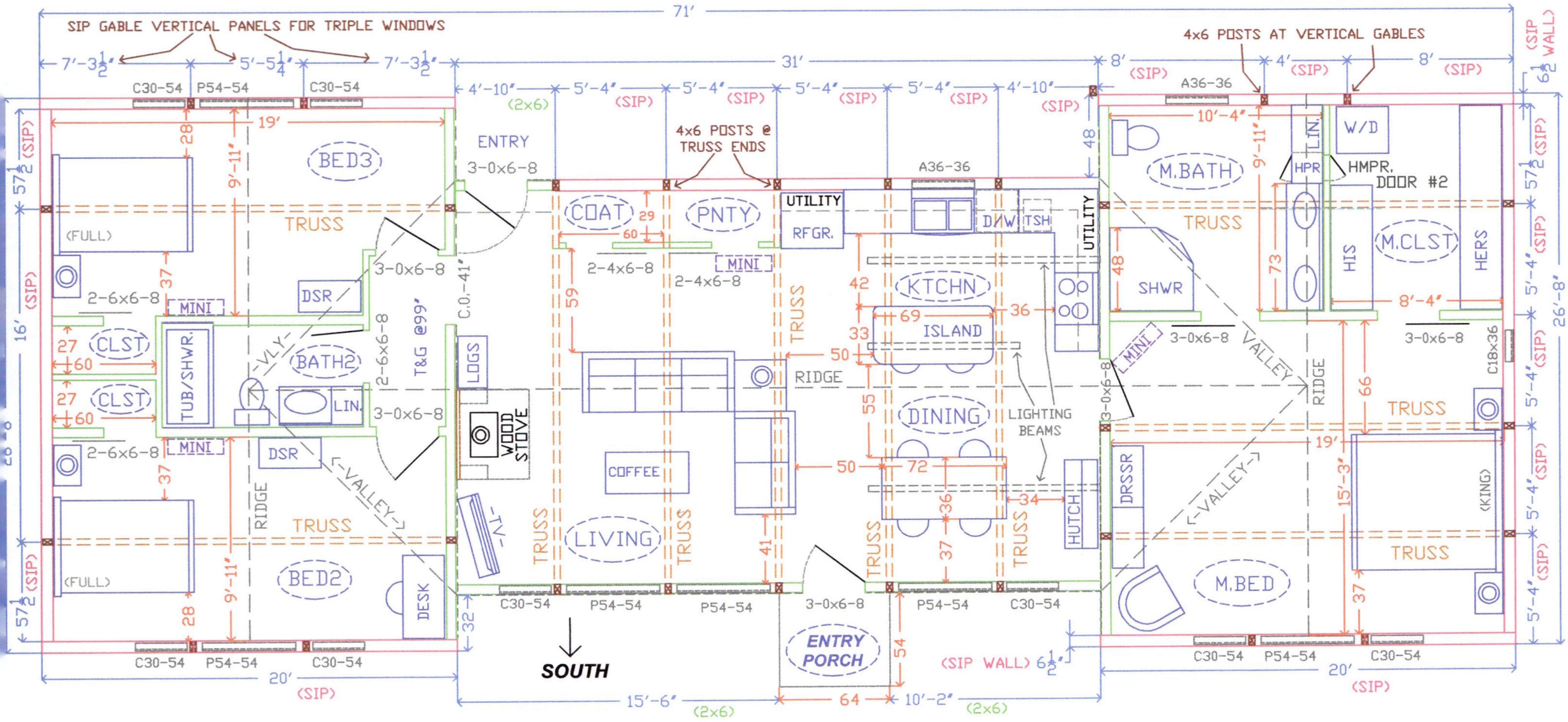

Fig. 7.3 Floor plan of Squashed-H

MISC. CONSTRUCTION NOTES:

- With two roof valley infill framing sets in this plan, using our "Modularity" strategy for pre-building those in a shop, with a tooling jig, similar to the earlier Gable top halves fabrication approach, is also smart production efficiency
- Note on the plan the unusual dimensions on the vertical gable SIPs with the triple window grouping. (Rather than the even simpler, generic, non-windowed 8', 4', and 8' pattern first shown.) To effectively use the triple window scheme in the gables, it is best to break the gap with two studs at the window opening plus one half of the vertical 4×6 post widths foam relief gap (like in the eave truss ends) for strength, particularly when lifting the fully assembled gable wall section as shown on the book cover picture. That specific gable design needs to match the chosen window supplier and includes their recommended rough opening (R.O.) dimensions. (To be detailed in the "shop" drawings for the chosen SIP vendor.)
- Note the example three "lighting beams" in the kitchen area. These can be the same 4×6 pine material for the wall posts, but long enough to meet the gable wall for electrical connections.
- A small routered slot in the top of the beam (3/4" ×3/4") with a 1×3 trim cap will hide the wiring on top. (Lighting beam feature can be also added in the "seating" area.)
- The flat ceiling pine T&G roof decking at 99" height in the hallway, second bath, and the last two closets is employed here. Again, a storage loft zone above that flat ceiling is obtained and a convenient access hatch to reach it is made.
- The "COAT" and "PANTRY" closets near the entry could be implemented using 4×4 pine posts tied into the truss collar beams with either excess 2×8 T&G (or 1×6s, etc.) in a timber-like style wall. (Rather than the typical stud framing with double *Sheetrock* wall sides style covering.)
- The likely location for the deck/patio outdoor space is in the "rear" of the picture.

FLOOR PLAN HIGHLIGHTS:

Great Room:

- The dramatic, exposed, five-truss scheme is again, central to this plan (note fig. 7.4 showing the view from the kitchen end, displaying most of the trusses).
- The two large picture windows (54") and the one 30" casement grouping near the living/seating zone is a premier feature.
- The seating area is also well-clustered around the corner TV location and still good viewing proximity to the wood stove.
- The larger dining table (now 6') zone near the other large picture and flanking casement window is also a solid feature (particularly if an excellent "view" results from the chosen property)
- With the dining table under two trusses, coupled with the noted "lighting beam" option, a relatively large "Hutch" spot near the window corner is available (even with the longer dining table).

Fig. 7.4 Kitchen end of Great Room

Kitchen highlights:

- As implied in the last picture, the kitchen follows our typical "L" pattern layout
- We strongly suggest a longer, narrower Island as indicated on the floor plan. This size/shape flows with the narrow 20'-truss scheme much better and the resulting longer 32'-long room. It also does not pinch the dining table zone that an "Australia" sized (too deep) unit would
- The utility chase to aid wiring, plumbing and mini-split HVAC cabling is here again.
- The pull-out trash tray again near the dead corner enables future access for other uses (Tankless hot water location?)

Master bedroom highlights:

- The twin Timber Trusses scheme is again dramatic in this very large, 16'×20' footprint (320 sq.ft.)
- As indicated in the upcoming Figure 7.5 picture
- The triple window scheme again is a key asset here (note: could expand the two, typical 30"-wide flaking casements into the 36" version).
- The additional small casement window (C18"×36") in the corner close to the likely bed location and near the Master Closet provides cross-ventilation (usually not available in smaller rooms)

Fig. 7.5 Dual-trussed very large master bedroom

Master bath highlights:

- Large enough now for at least the 48" version popular trapezoid shower, glass wall kits (or larger)
- The longer 6' double sink vanity also is a good fit
- Note the unique "magic hamper" scheme with the clothes hamper principal door in the bathroom side (see back door in closet)
- A wide, tall (84"?), linen cabinet space is also available near the clothes hamper corner
- More space here, in general, as implied with the generous shower/toilet spacing is evident

Master Closet Highlights:
- The dual side, "HERS" (larger) and "HIS" clothes sections fits well
- A stacked washer/dryer in the "HIS" side also leaves a gap for the "MAGIC Hamper" rear access door right near the washer/dryer
- The vaulted space above both clothe hanging zones, at the lower 7' height, provides two storage lofts

2nd bedroom highlights

- The single Timber Truss format provides an interesting long and narrow layout (see Figure 7.6)
- With likely street side view here, the triple-window-plan is a strong feature for a non-master type bedroom (could also upgrade with the wider 36" casements here)
- This, less-impacted-by-the-hallway room, enables a potential Mini-office/desk nook near the windows
- A respectable, 5'-wide, slightly deeper than typical 24", closet is also provided

THE "SQUASHED H" 101

Fig. 7.6 Single Timber Truss bedroom view

- The HVAC, indoor "Mini-split" location, utility needs works well with the closet/bath flat ceilinged T&G pine approach

3rd bedroom highlights:

- The single Timber Truss, long/narrow room layout is here again (Figure 7.6)
- The triple-window-plan is a very nice feature, even on the likely "rear of the house" location
- With the wider 36" casements again, a potential upgrade
- Impacted more by the hallway notch, a desk location near the windows is still doable
- A twin to the 2nd bedroom closet, is again provided
- The HVAC, indoor "Mini-split" location again capitalizes on the "utility running function" of the flat T&G ceilinged zone (plus the potential extra loft storage & convenient access hatch planning)

2nd bathroom highlights:

- The slightly larger than "apartment-size" layout does provide for a tall linen cabinet in the near door corner
- The longer length also allows more space between the toilet typically seen, plus a respectable 30"-wide, popular sized, sink vanity
- The normal 64"-wide gable structural wall/truss spacing (with only 58-1/2" net between, or 1-1/2" short) does cramp the typical 60" long tub. So either the 2×6 gables moved outward 1.5" (again, okay for the roof T&G joint overlaps**), the 2×4 section only at the tub base, or even the full 2×4 framed gable approach does provide even more space than shown

** Even this one-time 1-1/2" wall offset allows a 1-1/4"-wide nailing ledge for the T&G lengths, which also almost always have an extra 1/4" to 1/2". The "typical" framed roof, as in fig. 3.17 has only 3/4" of the one-half engineered truss or 2×s width to nail the thin, typical, 7/16" OSB sheathing mating ends.

Wrap up and conclusions:

Closing this work without the following two key functions would be too non-conclusive :
1. An epilogue update on the Walnut Mountain *EnergyStar* house featured in the earlier book.
2. My "favorites" from the half dozen floor plans here.

Ironically, I recently bumped into one of the two owners, at lunch, on the closing day of selling the Walnut house (great room picture in Fig. 1.2) after more than eleven years of content ownership. The two owners, at the purchase in 2007, had just "escaped" from a north Atlanta suburb to this quiet north Georgia mountain community. They were late in their working careers with retirement in the near future. Their original intent expanded the unfinished basement into about 2,800 sq.ft. total, finished, living space plus another 300 sq.ft. of unfinished storage. Effectively, they had created almost two distinct living "suite" levels on the completed home when moving in. Unfortunately, the still-working partner passed just before my lunch meeting. The second owner, now into retirement, (and single income level) was now not a fit for this relatively larger home. Her regretting final comment to me: "I wish that I had just the main floor!" (2 bed, 2 bath, 1,550 sq.ft. total)

And the new, confirmed, happy owner? They had also "escaped", but from a high-property-tax, New England state!

Now the process of me naming my "favorites" here is so akin to the classic choice that a parent sometimes confronts about "choosing their favorite child" (My only child is my "Favorite Daughter"!).

Thus, my best attempt here is to simply organize them into three general categories:

1. MOST PRACTICAL:

- "MINI" Vaulted Ranch (2 bedrooms, 2 baths, 960 total sq.ft.)
- "WING-ED" Chalet #2 (2 bedroom, 2 baths, 1,260 total sq.ft.)

2. PRACTICAL/MORE COMFORTABLE:

- "MAXI" Vaulted Ranch (2 bedrooms, 2 baths, 1,173 total sq.ft.)
- "TEE" Chalet (2 bed, 2 bath, 1,377 total sq.ft.)

3. MOST COMFORTABLE:

(and easy transition from late career living and then still use in retirement):
- "WINGED" Chalet #3 (3 bed, 2 bath, 1493 total square feet)
- "SQUASHED-H" (3 bedrooms, 2 baths, 1,700 total sq.ft.)

SO . . .
"THAT IS MY STORY, AND I AM STICKING TO IT!"

From Art Smith – somewhere near the north Georgia Appalachians. . .

REFERENCES

1. "Preface" from Homers Iliad, by Alexander Pope
2. Building with Structural Insulated Panels, by Michael Morley, Taunton Press
3. R-CONTROL SIP brochure : R-Control Building Systems, Excelsior, MN
4. www.sips.org, BASF Study shows Sips Cut Framing labor in Half", 2/13/2008
5. R-CONTROL SIP brochure : R-Control Building Systems, Excelsior, MN
6. 2006 International Residential Code, p268, 803.1
7. 2013 IECC (RESIDENTAIL ENERGY CODE)
8. MITSUBISHI ELECTRIC Submittal M-Series form: MXZ-3B24NA-1
9. The Passive Solar Energy Book, by Edward Mazria, Rodale, p402
10. The Passive Solar Energy Book, by Edward Mazria, Rodale, p138 & 139
11. Consumer Reports, August 2016
12. https://www.mikeroweworks.org/
13. https://neces.ed.gov/programs/digest/tables
14. Consumer Reports, August 2016, front cover
15. The Passive Solar Energy Book, by Edward Mazria, Rodale, p252
16. www.uscensus.gov, "Median and average Square feet…."

www.ingramcontent.com/pod-product-compliance
Lightning Source LLC
Chambersburg PA
CBHW061754290426
44108CB00029B/2986